WILL NURSES CALL THE SHOTS?

A Look at the Delivery of Health Care Twenty Years from Now

Ralph W. Sutherland, MD

1996

Available from the Canadian Nurses Association, 50 Driveway, Ottawa, ON K2P 1E2, Tel: (613) 237-2133 or 1-800-361-8404, Fax: (613) 237-3520; the Canadian Public Health Association, 1565 Carling Avenue, Suite 400, Ottawa, ON K1Z 8R1, Tel: (613) 725-3769, Fax: (613) 725-9826; many bookstores; and, from Ralph Sutherland, Box 129, Plevna, ON K0H 2M0, Tel: (613) 479-2325 or (613) 725-1299, Fax: (613) 729-0309

Price: $18.95

For one book ordered from Ralph Sutherland and not prepaid: add $4.00 for shipping and handling. No shipping or handling charges for prepaid orders or orders for more than one book.

Other books by the author:

Health care in Canada 1988 (With Jane Fulton) (out of print)

Spending Smarter and Spending Less: Policies and Partnerships for Health Care in Canada, 1994 (with Jane Fulton). Available from the Canadian Public Health Association, the Canadian Hospital Association and Ralph Sutherland. Price $39.00.

For purchase of both *Will Nurses Call the Shots?* and *Spending Smarter and Spending Less* - from Ralph Sutherland only - $45.00. No shipping and handling charges.

Canadian Cataloguing in Publication Data

Sutherland, Ralph W.
        Will nurses call the shots? : a look at health care delivery twenty years from now

Includes index.
ISBN 0-9681281-0-6

        1. Medical care--Canada. 2. Medical personnel--Canada.

RA449.S895   362.1'0971   C96-900722-1

Published by Ralph W. Sutherland

Design and layout by
Publications Department, Canadian Nurses Association, Ottawa, ON

Printed by Tri-Graphic, Ottawa, ON Canada

"Firmly held opinions are a luxury affordable only to those to whom outcomes do not matter."

Author unknown

Dedications

This book is dedicated to all health care professionals who provide cost-effective health care.

In particular, it is dedicated to three nurses.

The first nurse is Meg Breton, who, in the mid-1950s, joined the nursing staff of the small hospital in Eastend, Saskatchewan, in which I was practising. She very quickly taught me that an experienced midwife knew more about obstetrics than a well-trained Canadian general practitioner. Meg Breton showed me that society is not always fair in the privileges it grants, and she began (although neither of us knew it at the time) the process of showing me how competent specialized nurses can be.

The second nurse is Ross, my oldest son, who, after a very successful career in labour organizing and labour organizations (among other things), became an equally successful nurse. His knowledge and skill in hospital-based emergency medicine has confirmed the extent to which nurses can provide sophisticated health care when they work exclusively in one clinical field and constantly upgrade their skills.

The third nurse is Jeannette Bennett, who for eight years has worked as part of the primary care team at the Sandy Hill Community Health Centre in Ottawa. She (and dozens of other nurses in many locations) demonstrates daily the adequacy with which nurse practitioners can provide independent health care even when encumbered by anachronistic legislation. (In more recent years Jeannette has been the "significant other" in my life. Our next joint project will be a book on ethics in health care.)

Acknowledgements

Many people contributed to the evolution and the final revisions of this book. My thanks to all of them.

Special thanks are due to the nursing associations of New Brunswick, Nova Scotia and Newfoundland, to the Medical Association of Newfoundland and Labrador, and to the many representatives of the Departments of Health of New Brunswick, Nova Scotia and Newfoundland who met with me during my tour of the Atlantic provinces in late 1994 while working on this book.

Thanks also to the nursing faculty of Ryerson Polytechnical Institute and the University of Ottawa, who allowed me to discuss the book with them, and to the Canadian Nurses Association, Queen's University and the University of Ottawa for the use of their libraries.

Nora Brochu, Beatrice Mullington, Stephen Vail and others at the Canadian Nurses Association reviewed drafts of the manuscript and provided much useful information and comment. A draft of the book was also read by Karen Barclay, Ada Chambers, Jeannette Bennett, Brenda Shestowsky, Ross Sutherland and Professor Marjorie Robertson. Everyone provided valuable comment. My thanks to each of them.

Appreciation also goes to the publications department of the Canadian Nurses Association. They took the final draft through to its delivery to the printer, and they designed the cover.

Table of Contents

Chapter 4: Expanded roles for nurses   41

Chapter 5: Expanded use of existing health care professionals other than physicians and nurses   68

Chapter 6: The education options   76

Chapter 7: Funding and payment options and their effects on provider roles 91

Chapter 8: Opportunities for role expansions 99

List of Figures

List of Tables

Preamble

W ill Nurses Call the Shots? is a sequel to the book titled *Spending Smarter and Spending Less: Policies and Partnerships for Health Care in Canada*, Sutherland and Fulton, 1994.

Spending Smarter and Spending Less examined the big picture. It discussed the choices which are available to politicians, planners, administrators, providers, consumers and payers as they get ready for health care in the 21st century.

Spending Smarter and Spending Less discussed strategic planning questions. It discussed the organization, budgeting and regionalization of health care and the policy development process. It looked at how public decision making might be improved and how professional decision making can be improved. It discussed the tools available for control of public spending on health care. It did not, however, and could not, thoroughly examine all policy fields.

Will Nurses Call the Shots? examines one policy area which deserves more attention than it received in *Spending Smarter and Spending Less*, namely human resource issues in health care. *Will Nurses Call the Shots?* looks at how health care professionals are used and trained, and how both use and training might change.

This book struggles with many questions. Who will deliver health care in the 21st century? Will more health care professionals become independent practitioners? Who will be authorized to prescribe prescription drugs and order laboratory and other diagnostic tests? Who will be considered qualified to interpret test results? How many of the services once provided only by physicians will be provided by other professionals, and how will the other professionals be trained for their new functions? Will health care professions work in reasonable harmony? Will the dominance of physicians be preserved or will it be replaced by a more level playing field in which all professionals are able to do those things they are capable

Figure 1.1

Human Resource Problems in Health Care

The wrong person doing the job.

An unnecessary expansion of work (featherbedding).

Physician control over the scope of practice of other professionals.

Inadequate preparation of some providers.

No clear understanding as to who should deliver the new services which are constantly emerging.

Lack of cooperation among providers.

Provincial payment policies which encourage misuse of human resources.

Too little attention to maintaining competence.

Too little professional collaboration.

Most of the human resource issues listed in Figure 1.1 are discussed in this book. There is examination of the reasons for the current dominance of physicians. There is discussion of the options for change, and of the merits of the options. Evidence which supports a sharply expanded role for nurses in the delivery of health care is presented.

In the suggestions for change there are no hidden agendas. The only objective is to help the Canadian health care system become more cost-effective. Increasing or decreasing the image, or expanding or shrinking the future, of any specific health care professional is not a goal of this book, although such changes will occur if the suggestions made are implemented. There is no wish to be insensitive to the concerns of professionals whose job security, self-image and careers may be altered – but the concerns and interests of those who use health care, and who pay for it, must come first.

Throughout the book, major attention is devoted to policies and processes which will reduce the use of physician specialists.

Only minimal examination is given to the use of lower-cost personnel (aides and assistants) in nursing, physiotherapy, pharmacy, etc.

The field of dentistry receives almost no attention. This omission reflects the author's background much more than the importance of dentistry.

Throughout the book, terminology sometimes interferes with a simple and understandable examination of the issues.

For example, references are made to the "medical model". This term, as with many others, means different things to different people.

Some writers define the "medical model" as health care delivery in which technological curative services dominate and health promotion, prevention and caring are given inadequate attention. By contrast, in this book "medical model" refers to the historical, hierarchical, paternalistic and physician-dominated arrangement in which:
- physicians are the undisputed head of the medical care team;
- the opinions of physicians are given more weight than the opinions of other health care professionals;
- physicians have major (or complete) control over the extent to which "medical" activities are performed by other health care professionals;
- evaluation of physicians is performed only by other physicians;
- physician opinions override the opinions of consumers;
- physicians control the education and evaluation of other health care professionals working within the model;
- physicians establish their own rates of pay.

The first two features of the "medical model" (as described above) still largely apply; the last three are gone; the status of the middle two is changing. None of the listed characteristics of the medical model are defensible, but the laws which exist in most provinces continue to preserve portions of the medical model and some of the associated special privileges for physicians.

"Medical model" is not the only confusing term. Nursing titles are a mess. Writers refer to clinical nurse specialists, clinical nurse specialist/nurse practitioners, nurse clinicians, nurse practitioners, advanced practice nurses and extended class nurses. There are also clinically specific titles such as public health nurse, lactation consultant, incontinence advisor, case manager, nurse midwife and nurse anesthetist. Many terms are used differently by different programs, authors and locations. Differences may be rooted in the educational programs from which the professionals graduated or in provincial, institutional or local preferences.

No attempt will be made to define primary, secondary and tertiary health care beyond the vague proposition that primary care is usually the least complex and is usually delivered by the first provider that the patient sees. Secondary and tertiary care are more likely to be complex, be provided by a specialist and be provided on referral. The terms primary, secondary and tertiary care will seldom be used, but when used they should be understood to be fuzzy and indistinct.

No distinction will be made between primary care, primary medical care and primary health care, although a distinction is sometimes made by other writers and by some professionals, especially in the nursing literature.

The terms technician and technologist are considered to be interchangeable.

This book is written for all who are interested in the way health care is delivered. By virtue of its major attention to the future roles of nurses, it may be of special interest to them.

The book is built around two hypotheses. The first is that expensive professionals (especially specialist physicians) are very regularly used to provide services which could be adequately provided at a lower cost by other providers. The second hypothesis is that expanded roles for less expensive providers, especially nurses, are no longer experimental.

To some readers, this book will deal with the process of human re-engineering, i.e., the process of altering the roles of individuals in the performance of work. This buzzword will not be used, but human re-engineering is definitely the subject.

To other readers, much of the book will be seen to deal with issues associated with labour adjustment. This also is correct. Many of the human resource management issues discussed are similar to those which have been examined as governments and employers have struggled with changes in health care. Many provinces (e.g., British Columbia, Quebec and Ontario) have created commissions, committees and processes to reduce the turmoil associated with alterations in how and where health care is delivered. The work done by these agencies will be valuable in provinces which decide to transfer functions to less expensive personnel.

The book has twelve chapters. Chapter 1 describes the many ways in which the utilization of health care professionals has changed, and why these changes have occurred. Chapter 2 describes recent changes in the organization, financing, cost control, evaluation and delivery of health care. Chapter 3 sets out some of the human resource policy options which are available to each province. Chapters 4 to 7 examine the various policy options. Chapter 8 summarizes the evidence which supports the proposition that much of what physicians do, especially specialist physicians, ought to be done by less expensive personnel. Chapter 9 reviews the policy development (policy analysis) process. Chapters 10 and 11 discuss what should be done by governments and by nurses (respectively) to implement the changes which appear to be desirable.

Why Professional Roles Change

The services being provided today by doctors, nurses, physiotherapists and other health care providers are not the same as the services which were being provided a few decades ago. There have been changes in what is done, how it is done and who it is done by. Changes have occurred in primary, secondary and tertiary care, in health promotion, disease prevention, diagnosis, therapy and rehabilitation, and in mental health, physical health and psychosocial health.

Chapter 1 examines the way the roles and powers of health care professionals have evolved over the last half-century. An understanding of this evolution will help Canadians choose the future changes which are most practical and acceptable, and will help those who must implement the changes.

Many factors have contributed to the changes which have occurred in the roles of health care professionals. These factors include politics, public policy, the decisions of physicians, public pressure, a search for lower costs, competition, methods of payment, protection of income, technological developments, provider imagination, the emergence of new needs, shortages of personnel and changes in the organization and delivery of health care.

The influence of public policy on professional roles

Each province has the constitutional authority to define the roles of health care workers in that province.

Using their constitutional authority, each province many decades ago gave physicians the exclusive right to provide medical care and gave dentists similar powers in dentistry. Other professions could provide medical care only with the agreement of physicians, and they could provide dental care only with the agreement of dentists.

Governments, on occasion, have not approved of the manner in which physicians and dentists used their ability to control the scope of practice of other professionals. When this happened, each province passed more laws. For example, special statutes were passed to give chiropractors and optometrists exemption from physician control. Similar statutes allowed denturists to provide denture services directly to the public and allowed dental therapists in Saskatchewan to do fillings, install crowns and extract baby teeth.

Besides the laws giving overriding general powers and rights to allopathic physicians, or which exempt certain professionals from physician control, all provinces have legislation pertaining specifically to nurses, physiotherapists and other health care professionals. These laws allow the affected professions to be self-governing, but they do not authorize provision of "medical care." The scope of practice of nurses, physiotherapists and other professionals working within the medical model remains (in all provinces but Ontario) largely under physician control.

Besides direct statutory control over the roles and relationships of health care professionals, provinces through their public policies also affect roles indirectly. The reorientation of mental health services from institutional care to community care, for example (a reorientation which is the product of public policy) increases the extent to which social workers, psychiatric nurses, public health nurses and psychologists are the first point of contact for users.

A new Ontario statute illustrates the dominant role which public policy can have in determining the roles of health care professionals. This statute is such a major departure from earlier statutes that it will be discussed at some length.

The (Ontario) Regulated Health Professions Act (RHPA)

The RHPA was the product of seven years of work by the Schwartz Commission. The goals of the Schwartz Commission were improved public protection, greater professional openness and accountability, improved quality of care and more choices for consumers.

The Schwartz Commission decided that no profession should determine the scope of practice of any other profession. ("Scope of practice" is the range of services which a profession is legally able to deliver.)

The Commission recommended changes in the degree to which Ontario physicians and dentists have exclusive rights to deliver care. It proposed that the powers, responsibilities and scope of practice of each health care profession should be defined in law and that changes in these roles, responsibilities and powers should be directly under the control of the provincial Minister of Health.

The Schwartz Commission identified thirteen activities (or types of activities) in health care which, in their opinion, required special skills and/or judgment. The Commission recommended that these activities be "controlled" in the sense that only specified professionals would be authorized to provide them or to delegate them to others.

Any activity not identified as a "controlled act" could be performed by anyone. A physical examination and the taking of a medical history, for example, were not identified as controlled acts and therefore could be performed by anyone.

The report of the Schwartz Commission led to the RHPA and to related separate statutes governing self-regulating professions. The Acts were passed in 1991 and proclaimed on January 1, 1994. (The intervening two and one-half years were spent developing regulations for the many Acts.)

The RHPA is an umbrella statute. It sets out principles and processes and establishes mechanisms.

The RHPA was passed in association with 21 separate "professions Acts", each titled "An Act respecting the regulation of the profession of...". These Acts govern 24 professions including 17 which were previously self-regulating under the Health Disciplines Act (allopathic physicians, chiropractors, dentists, dental hygienists, denture therapists, dental technologists, massage therapists, nurses, nursing assistants, ophthalmic dispensers, optometrists, osteopaths, pharmacists, physiotherapists, podiatrists and chiropodists, psychologists and radiological technicians) and seven which acquired self-governing status for the first time in Ontario (audiologists, dieticians, medical laboratory technicians, occupational therapists, respiratory therapists/technologists, speech language pathologists and midwives). Another 55 occupational groups were assessed and did not meet the criteria required for self-regulation. The most important criteria were the presence of a definable scope of practice and of defined standards of practice.

Each "professions Act" governs at least one self-governing profession. Each Act creates one or more professional College(s), defines the scope of practice of the governed profession(s) and describes the responsibilities of the profession(s). Podiatrists and chiropodists share an Act but have separate Colleges. The same applies to audiologists and speech language pathologists. Registered Nurses and Registered Practical Nurses (formerly Registered Nursing Assistants) are governed by the same professional Act and the same College.

The professional Acts indicate which of the controlled acts can be performed by each profession. Often a "controlled act" is within the scope of practice of a profession but only in specified circumstances, e.g., podiatrists and chiropodists are authorized to perform injections but only on the feet. (The "controlled acts" which can be performed in Ontario by each profession are summarized in the Appendix, Table 13.1.)

With the proclamation of the RHPA no profession in Ontario has legal control over the scope of practice of any other profession. The determination of scope of practice is now directly under the control of the Minister of Health, who is advised by a Regulated Health Professions Advisory Council. The mandate of the Advisory Council is to recommend which professions should be regulated or unregulated, suggest amendments to Acts and Regulations, and monitor the quality assurance and patient relations programs of each of the professional Colleges. The Minister is obliged to refer substantive changes in the Acts or their Regulations to the Advisory Council for advice, but the final decision rests entirely with the Minister. A profession seeking expanded roles makes its case directly to the Advisory Council and the Minister.

The RHPA significantly decreased the power of physicians and increased opportunities for other professionals. Although there have been few immediate changes in the way health care is delivered in Ontario, a new power balance and a more level playing field have been created.

The principles of the RHPA are of interest to many provinces. A January 1992 meeting of the provincial Ministers of Health recommended elimination of exclusive fields of practice. This agreement in principle does not mean that the details of the Ontario legislation will be replicated in other provinces, but it indicates that major change is under consideration everywhere. The March 1993 document, *Creating a Climate for Change: Physician Policy Development in Nova Scotia*, states "The Task Force has accepted in general the need to explore the effective utilization of health care professionals, including the realignment of roles and changes in the regulation of health professionals." (p. 71) In the future, many services formerly provided only by physicians will become available from other professionals. Physicians and dentists in all provinces will lose control over the scope of practice of other professionals.

Despite the 1992 support of the provincial Ministers of Health for the elimination of exclusive fields of practice, only Ontario has introduced comprehensive new legislation. (Even with this change in legislation the power of physicians continues to be felt. The

Council which advises the Minister of Health of Ontario regarding changes in the roles of other professionals [such as nurse practitioners] has, to date, largely accepted the advice of physicians.)

Legislation similar to the RHPA in Ontario has been considered in the United States. In November 1993, The Health Security Act was introduced in Congress. This Act would have, if passed, prevented any State from requiring that any professional be supervised by any other. The intent was to foster competition between physicians and other health care professionals, especially nurse specialists. (Jenkins, S.M., "Health Care Reform: Antitrust and Competitive Implications for Nursing", *AAOHN*, February 1994, pp. 89-93.)

The RHPA does not prevent a profession from delegating functions to other professionals, but these delegations cannot offend the RHPA or its associated professional Acts. Physicians will, in the future as in the past, delegate functions to nurses and others when it is in their interests to do so.

Physician influence over the roles of other health care professionals

Physicians in all Canadian provinces except Ontario are still legally able to prevent most health care professionals from delivering medical care. Physicians also have the authority to delegate the delivery of a "medical" service to someone else. This capacity to prevent growth in the scope of practice of other professionals, combined with the authority to delegate when deemed desirable, has made physician decisions a major determinant of what many other professionals are legally able to do.

Delegation first became common during the Second World War, when the roles of nurses, laboratory technicians and others who worked under the supervision of physicians were markedly expanded. Increased delegation to other workers (of duties which were formerly performed by physicians) was a product of both necessity and common sense. There were too few physicians and too much work, and other providers were available.

It was in the interest of physicians, especially in the armed forces, to delegate duties to other professionals. The delegation did not lead to a drop in physician incomes, did not break the law, acknowledged the inherent abilities of nurses and others, and made it possible for more care to be delivered. The changes were a product of innovative caregivers responding to new challenges, new technologies and the absence of payment by fee-for-service. Doctors, other health care providers and patients were all winners.

After the Second World War, physician associations began to formally examine the question of which "medical acts" should be delegated to nurses and others. Physicians quickly recognized that delegating responsibilities to other professionals could reduce physician access to patients and income. The transfer of activities to other professionals was, in the civilian setting, not so welcomed as had been the case in a military setting.

When physicians did not approve of the delegation of a particular "medical" act to nurses or others, the other professionals could not legally perform that function regardless of their training or experience. For example, a midwife from Europe could not, in Canada, deliver the obstetrical care she had delivered in Europe. This was the case even when the midwife had obstetrical skills which were superior to those of the average Canadian family physician.

A pattern soon emerged. Only services with selected characteristics were delegated to other professionals. Physicians approved the delegation of duties to other professionals when: (a) the activity or service was one which physicians did not wish to perform; and/or (b) the delegation did not reduce physician income; and/or (c) the service being delegated could be billed for by a physician if performed by someone employed by the physician. Physicians accepted changes, or promoted them, when the changes made the physician's work day more manageable without threatening income.

Many examples illustrate the pattern of delegation of "medical" acts to other professionals.

Prior to the early 1940s, all types of injections were given by physicians. The appearance of aqueous penicillin, however, required intramuscular injections every three hours around the clock. Physicians immediately delegated intramuscular injections to nurses.

Until the 1950s, microscopic examination of tissue samples (from lung, cervix, skin, etc.) was performed almost entirely by pathologists and selected laboratory technicians. With the introduction of cervical cytology screening programs for the detection of the early stages of cervical cancer, however, there were suddenly thousands of specimens to be examined. Pathologists could not have examined all of these specimens even if they had wanted to, and they didn't want to. One option was to have the specimens examined by laboratory technologists, but there were also not enough technologists and they also did not want this boring task. Almost overnight, the screening of cervical smears was delegated to a new health care worker. Special educational programs offering one year or less of training after high school produced cervical cytology technicians. These technicians were trained to do a preliminary screening of the cervical smears. (Specimens which might be abnormal were, and still are, referred to more trained personnel for additional assessment.)

In the 1980s it became necessary to routinely measure blood gases in large numbers of patients. This required the frequent and around-the-clock collection of samples of arterial blood. Prior to the routine measurement of blood gases, the collection of a specimen of arterial blood was considered to be too dangerous and difficult to be performed by anyone but a physician. In the face of high-volume and unscheduled demands, however, physicians rapidly decided that arterial blood specimens should be collected by someone else. The collection of arterial blood specimens by nurses and technicians is now routine in many hospitals. (Dettenmeier, P.A., *Pulmonary Nursing Care*, Mosby, 1992.) In some hospitals, nurses also evaluate the blood gas findings and act on them.

Physicians, acting through their provincial organizations or a hospital medical staff, or on an individual basis, have delegated many specific medical tasks to nurses, paramedics, office staff and a variety of other workers. Delegation by a hospital medical staff or by an individual physician is usually unchallenged whether or not it has been approved by a provincial medical association.

Leaving decisions at the local level allows different groups of physicians to make different decisions. Physicians in one hospital may wish to act as surgical assistants or apply their own plaster casts; the medical staff of another hospital may prefer to delegate these activities to other professionals.

The delegation of physician tasks and responsibilities to other professionals is accelerating, partly in response to reductions in the number of medical residents (physicians in training). Nurses now provide many services formerly provided by residents.

Besides activities mentioned earlier, the list of tasks delegated by physicians to someone else includes the drawing of blood, the administration of tuberculosis skin tests, immunization, rectal and vaginal examinations during pregnancy, suturing, the administration of selected drugs, pronouncing patients dead, external cardiac massage and defibrillation.

The delegation of functions by physicians to other professionals has varied somewhat by province. Until the 1970s, Ontario doctors provided all immunization in public health immunization clinics, whereas this became a nursing function in western provinces in the 1950s. Transfer of this activity to Ontario nurses was delayed for 10 to 20 years in Ontario to avoid elimination of a source of physician income. The events in Ontario reflected the greater doctor supply in Ontario.

Early expansions in nurse functions were often introduced by physicians without consultation with the nurses affected. This led to objections from nursing associations. Nurses complained that they were being asked to perform duties for which they had not been trained. In response to these complaints, joint nurse/physician committees were established. These consultation mechanisms continue to be used.

Physicians (and dentists) have, on a number of occasions, refused to delegate activities to other professionals or to support the existence of the other professionals. Allopathic physicians (Canadian medical school graduates are all allopathic physicians) have successfully prevented osteopathic physicians from being licensed in Canada. The recognition which was given to osteopathic physicians in the United States decades ago has not arrived in Canada.

Physicians fought vigorously against the licensing of chiropractors. Physicians were unable to prevent eventual legitimization of chiropractic care, but in some provinces physician opposition delayed recognition for decades.

Physicians have greatly delayed legal recognition of midwives. It is only in the last few years that Canadian provinces have begun to ignore physician objections and recognize the profession which delivers most of the babies in many countries with maternal and infant mortality statistics equal to or better than Canada. In 1994, midwives with specified attributes became independent practitioners in Ontario. They have prescribing authority, hospital admitting privileges, new training programs and provincial funding for their services.

Physicians often indulge in circuitous and strange rituals as they seek to distance themselves from midwives. Anesthetists wonder whether they should provide anesthesia services to a patient being delivered by a midwife. Obstetricians wonder how they should react to a referral from a midwife. The fact that physicians in Europe and elsewhere resolved these issues long ago seems not to reassure Canadian physicians who are looking for trouble.

In general, physicians object to anyone who competes for patients and dollars. In Manitoba, the 1991 Provincial Advisory Committee on Midwifery brought forward a report which proposed a tentative introduction of midwifery but which made it clear that the funds available to physicians should not go down as midwives were introduced. (The majority of the Committee were physicians.)

Misinformation from physicians is not limited to comments regarding midwives. There continue to be physician claims that nurse practitioners have not been proven to be as competent as physicians. (Kassirer, J.K., Editorial, *NEJM*, January 20, 1994.) In the Medical Post of March 15, 1994, Dr. Rick Mann, President of the Ontario Chapter of the College of Family Physicians, is quoted as saying that nurse practitioners will jeopardize quality of care and that they should not practice as independent practitioners.

Medical leaders should know better. Many reports have confirmed the equivalency of nurse practitioners and family physicians in many situations. ("The Burlington Randomized Trial of Nurse Practitioners", *NEJM*, 1974, pp. 251-256; "A meta-analysis of process of care, clinical outcomes, and cost-effectiveness of nurses in primary care roles: Nurse practitioners and nurse midwives", American Nurses Association, December 1992; "Report of the United States Office of Technology Assessment", 1992) In the Burlington Randomized Trials nurse practitioners were found to be able to do 90% of what family physicians do with equal outcomes and lower cost.

The 1992 American Nurses Association report referenced in the preceding paragraph reviewed 900 documents which compared the services of physicians and nurses. Fifty-three of the reports were considered to have scientific merit. Twelve used a randomized design. In general, nurse and physician prescribing volumes were similar, nurses ordered more laboratory tests, nurses spent more time on health promotion, nurses tended to score higher on measures of quality and nurse outcomes were superior. The number of visits was similar but nurse visits were 50% longer than those of physicians. Nurse patients had fewer hospitalizations. Nurse costs were lower, but financial findings in the United States may not be transferable to Canada where physician incomes are significantly lower.

The conduct of physicians usually illustrates a high degree of self-interest, but the medical community also has wonderful bright spots. In Ontario, as the midwife discussions proceeded, obstetricians in Hamilton reported that they had already worked successfully with midwives for a number of years without chaos, without patient hazard and without physician exposure to legal action (*Ontario Medical Review*, July 1994). The potential for collaboration between the professions has also been proven in Community Health Centres. (Way, D.O., and L.M. Jones, "The Family Physician – Nurse Practitioner Dyad: Indications and Guidelines", *CMAJ*, July 1, 1994.)

Individual dentists and physicians have, at times, promoted expanded roles for other professionals, or new relationships with other professionals, even when faced with colleague opposition. Innovative and courageous individual ophthalmologists pioneered partnerships with optometrists, a partnership in which refractions ceased to be part of the role of the ophthalmologist. Dentists who supervised dental therapists in New Zealand and later in the Saskatchewan children's dental program in the 1960s and 1970s accepted and legitimized the delivery of dental care by persons other than dentists. Open-minded physiatrists have created and worked in rehabilitation teams in which a variety of rehabilitation workers fully utilized their skills. Individual psychiatrists promoted psychiatric teams, especially in the community, in which nurses and social workers became the primary first-contact mental health workers. A recent report by the directors of family medicine departments in Ontario universities stated that "nonphysicians, especially nurses, are underused and undervalued in the primary care system". (*Canadian Family Physician*, September 1994.)

Opposition to change is usually expressed as concern regarding quality or cost. Opponents claim that there is not enough proof that the changes are reasonable and practical. However the opposition is expressed, it is often primarily a question of someone protecting their own interests.

As early as 1897 physicians objected to the emergence of the Victorian Order of Nurses (VON). Dire consequences for patients were predicted if nurses were allowed to provide home care. Physicians have not changed much in the last 99 years.

Physicians have not only affected the evolution of the roles of other health care professionals; they have affected the roles of each other. The power of specialist physicians, for example, has reduced family physician roles in many clinical fields such as obstetrics, surgery and anesthesia (Figure 2.1, p. 30). Reductions in opportunities to provide some services have been offset by greater involvement of family physicians in other activities such as psychotherapy, marriage and family counselling, eye testing (refractions), acting as surgical assistants, acupuncture and physiotherapy.

The role of other professions in change

Many professions have contributed to the changes in professional roles.

Pharmacists led in the evolution of the pharmacist assistant, a change which has reduced pharmacist involvement in the counting of pills. Nursing associations have at times approved, and at other times have disapproved, of the transfer of nursing activities to less-skilled nursing personnel. Until recently, physiotherapists did not approve of formally trained physiotherapy assistants.

Dentists approved of the use of dental hygienists, but only when working under the supervision of dentists. Dentists opposed the appearance of independent denturists and dental therapists.

Professional parochialism as a factor in change

Health care professionals (of all types) often fail to appreciate the simplicity of many of the things they do. They often see themselves as having unique skills when the skills are, in fact, either found in other workers or could be present in other workers.

Nurses, for example, tend to believe they are the logical profession to educate the public and promote health, but many other professionals such as teachers, police officers, social workers and public health inspectors also participate in health education, disease prevention, accident prevention and health promotion of all other types.

Many physicians believe that only they are adequately prepared to diagnose and prescribe treatment, and that only they can competently "communicate a diagnosis to a patient". This despite the fact that most health care professionals routinely and competently diagnose, prepare care plans and carry out the plans, and that these professionals must and do competently involve consumers in discussions of diagnoses and their implications.

Some health care professionals consider their skills and the uniqueness of their professional challenges to be so great that administrators and planners who are not members of the appropriate profession are considered to be inherently unable to "understand". The solution the health care professionals promote is to have health care professionals become administrators and planners whether or not they have adequate preparation for administration and planning. Medical Officers of Health, and the statutes which protect them, are an example. Clinical public health, epidemiology and research dominate most of the university programs which train public health physicians (Quebec is an exception) but finance, policy, information systems, program implementation, labour relations and personnel skills are central to the responsibilities of most Medical Officers of Health. Nurses often consider Schools of Nursing to be the best place to educate senior nurse managers and planners despite the fact that management and planning are not part of the central expertise of most nursing faculties.

Some professionals continue to preserve and almost cherish barriers between themselves and other professionals. Many physicians and physiotherapists still consider chiropractors to be hazardous, and communication between these professionals is next to nil.

Optometrists were, for many years, also officially unacceptable to physicians. Communication and cooperation are now much improved. Ophthalmologists at the University of Saskatchewan have, for 30 years, had optometrists working with them. Other sources of eye care, including the private ophthalmological clinics in Alberta, now use teams of ophthalmologists and optometrists.

Despite evidence that the physician dominated hierarchical model of health care is out of date and does not allow full use of the skills of all members of the health care team, many physicians still consider all other professionals within the medical model to be at least one step below themselves. In 1985-86, the British Columbia Medical Association commissioned a series of 26 television programs (at a cost of $2 million) to acquaint the public with the health care system. Over 90 different physicians participated, but there was no significant attention to providers other than physicians. This may be understandable considering that the programs were paid for by physicians, but it may also reflect an inaccurate perception by physicians of the modern health care team.

Financial factors

Cost has led to changes in roles. The prospect of providing services at lower cost contributed to expanded use of semi-skilled nursing staff and the introduction of pharmacist's assistants. The same prospect will, in the future, encourage expanded roles for nurses and other health care professionals.

Fee-for-service as the method of payment for physicians has reduced physician delegation of functions to other health care professionals. Delegation has usually not occurred if it prevented physicians from billing for the transferred service. The utilization of nurses and other professionals is broader when physicians are on salary (as in Community Health Centres) or payment is by capitation (as in the Health Maintenance Organizations in the United States).

Provincial health care insurance policies have had a great effect on how health care providers are used. Provincial medicare programs guarantee payments to physicians for the provision of a very broad spectrum of services. Provincial funding is not so routinely available for services provided by social workers, psychologists, audiologists, acupuncturists, osteopathic physicians, physiotherapists, dieticians, midwives, clinical nurse specialists and others. These exclusions occur even when the other professionals are at least as qualified as (and sometimes more qualified than) allopathic physicians. Absence of insurance coverage has prevented the full utilization of the skills of many health care professionals.

Changes in education

The education of nurses illustrates the fluidity of educational programs. Some of these changes have contributed to changes in how nurses are used.

Forty years ago, almost all nurses were trained in programs based in acute treatment hospitals. The nursing skills obtained were primarily the skills needed for employment in acute treatment hospitals. Nurses who wished to work in public health tended to go on to a one-year certificate course in that field. Nurses who wished to work in provincial psychiatric hospitals often enrolled in psychiatric nursing programs.

By the 1980s, most hospital-based nursing schools had closed. Most nurses became graduates of community college programs with a minority being baccalaureate graduates. Because the academic setting was not dominated by acute treatment hospitals, the RN programs strengthened attention to community and psychiatric nursing. With the strengthening of community nursing experience in the RN programs, some diploma public health nursing programs were discontinued. (Considering the present need for greater numbers of independent and skilled community nurses, reduced access to training in this important specialty stream may be unfortunate.)

The education and training of professionals other than nurses has also changed.

Programs which were at one time designed and supervised by physicians (e.g., the programs which train laboratory and radiology technologists) are now based in community colleges or universities. The standards and curriculum are now chosen by the educational institution and the professions involved.

Only a few years ago, one year of rotating interneship (after getting an MD) was all that was required to obtain a license to practice in any province. Physicians now face three years of mandatory training before licensure in most provinces.

Other factors which have affected the roles of health care providers

Public policy, professional decisions (especially those made by physicians) and money are the dominant determinants of the manner in which health care professionals are used, but other factors also play a role. These other factors include technological change, human resource shortages, new forms of health care organization, public opinion, competition and improved health care planning.

Technological developments have led to many changes. Cervical cytology screening led to the creation of a new type of technician. The threat of antibiotic-resistant bacteria led to the creation of specialists in infection control. Increased understanding of the chemistry and dynamics of respiration and blood gases led to the emergence of the respiratory therapist. Gene identification has led to new types of technologists and expanded roles for ethicists. Technology has fuelled open heart surgery, renal dialysis and tissue transplants and all of their associated special personnel.

Technology has sometimes simplified the duties of health care personnel and sometimes has made these duties more complex. Computerized Axial Tomography (CAT Scan), Magnetic Resonance Imaging (MRI), Positron Emission Tomography (PET), lithotripsy and angioplasty, for example, represent sophisticated new technologies which demand new skills. The automated developing of Xray films, on the other hand, reduced the skill required to produce an X-ray film, and newer anesthetics with fewer risks and more rapid recovery made anesthesia and surgery simpler and safer.

Some technologies have expanded the roles and the training of physician specialists. Other technologies have increased the feasibility of transferring activities to persons with less training.

Nurse shortages led to strengthened training and roles for semiskilled nursing personnel. An accelerated migration of Canadian physician specialists to the United States (*Ontario Medical Review*, July 1994 and February 1996) may hasten the replacement of specialist physicians by other professionals.

The emergence of community health centres gave nurse practitioners a friendly milieu for provision of the services they had been trained to provide. These opportunities could not emerge in fee-for-service offices.

Public pressure contributed to the legitimization of midwives, independent denturists and chiropractors, but user acceptance is not usually important in determining how health care provider roles change. Users almost always accept changes which health care professions and institutions choose to implement. Users may not even be aware that a change has occurred.

Competition has been only a minor factor in determining the roles of health care professionals. Competition from chiropractors may have contributed to an increased interest by physicians and physiotherapists in musculo-skeletal manipulation.

Changes may occur only when events demand a change, or those in charge may look ahead and plan. Most delegation of activities by physicians to other professionals has been reactive, as with the administration of penicillin or the taking of samples of arterial blood. Government action is a̶ ally reactive, as with the legitimization of chiropractors nd denturists. On occasion, changes have been well pl. he emergence of dental therapists in Saskatchewan in

Defining scope of practice

Two options are available when de nding the scope of practice of a profession.

One option is narrow and precise. I preserves a strong relationship between the work a professional does and the services that professional is authorized to provide.

The other option is more open-ended. It preserves only a very general (and often very weak) relationship between the services which a professional provides and the services the professional is authorized to provide.

The open-ended approach to defining scope of practice is best illustrated by the statutes and regulations which govern physicians. All physicians are authorized to deliver all medical care, and medical care is broadly defined.

The open-ended scope of practice allows physicians who practice quite differently to be governed by a single statute, a single set of regulations and a single professional college. Ophthalmologists, orthopedic surgeons, psychiatrists, family physicians, etc., all function under one set of rules.

An open-ended scope of practice has a down side to it. It authorizes professionals to perform or order services for which they have minimal if any training. For example, the Regulated Health Professions Act in Ontario allows all physicians to perform refractions, provide physiotherapy, perform spinal manipulation and perform brain surgery, but most physicians do not have skills in these areas. (Most physicians also do not provide these services.) All specialist physicians are legally able to perform the full range of medical services, but most have skills only within their specialty (and most provide services only within their specialty).

When governed by an open-ended scope of practice providers may make decisions or provide services outside of their areas of expertise. For example, in Ontario hearing aids can be prescribed by all physicians and all audiologists, but only audiologists and a limited number of physicians have the skill and knowledge required to determine which type of hearing aid is required.

When a hearing aid is prescribed by an audiologist, or by a physician competent in assessing hearing loss, the prescription gives specific instructions to the retailer who sells hearing aids. The retailer supplies the prescribed piece of equipment in the same way that a pharmacist fills a pharmaceutical prescription. When physicians do not have the competence to define the type of hearing aid needed, they can, if they wish, (and they usually do) write an imprecise prescription, e.g., "for a hearing aid please".

When the prescription is imprecise, an employee of the retailer, usually an audiologist, decides whether a hearing aid is necessary and what type should be prescribed. An agent of the company selling the hearing aid examines the patient, makes a diagnosis, advises as to the type of hearing aid that should be bought, and makes the sale. (*Ontario Medical Review*, June 1994, p. 21; *Members Dialogue*, CPSO, March 1994.) The situation is equivalent to a physician writing a pharmaceutical prescription which says to the pharmacist "for drug therapy please". An open-ended prescription may expose the consumer to exploitation.

The variance between the legal scope of practice of every physician and the range of competency of individual physicians is widely recognized. A patient in British Columbia who sued an ophthalmologist for having failed to notice mental illness lost her case because the judge ruled that it was not reasonable to expect an ophthalmologist to diagnose mental illness. (*Medical Post*, November 7, 1995, p. 28.)

The recently passed Regulated Health Professions Act in Ontario can be seen to encourage flexibility in the way scope of practice is described. *The 1995 Annual Report of the Ontario College of Physicians and Surgeons* describes the focus of the Regulated Health Professions Act as follows:

> "Under the RHPA... there is a new reliance and focus on monitoring how practitioners perform in practice rather than restricting their scopes of practice to areas for which they are nominally qualified. The effectiveness of this system will vary directly with the effectiveness of the performance monitoring process of each College." (p. 18)

The extent to which an open-ended scope of practice exposes the public to hazard is unclear. It is clear that many family physicians deliver services for which they have had little if any training, e.g., psychotherapy, acupuncture, refractions and physiotherapy. This suggests that an open-ended scope of practice is a hazard. On the other hand, the abuses can be considered to be present but not in sufficient quantity to merit concern. It can also be argued that other devices adequately lessen public risk. It can be assumed that personal ethics, hospital medical staff bylaws and the surveillance of the College of Physicians and Surgeons protect the public.

The alternative to an open-ended scope of practice is a narrow one. A narrow scope of practice clearly defines the range of clinical actions and decisions which a profession is authorized to perform.

Many professionals practice within a narrow scope of practice. Optometrists, for example, are restricted to the provision of services related to the eye and to only specified services. Chiropodists and podiatrists are authorized to care only for feet. They are (in Ontario) authorized to cut into subcutaneous tissues of the foot, to administer (by injection into feet) substances designated in the regulations, and to prescribe drugs designated in the regulations. The substances to be injected or prescribed can be listed reasonably easily because the work of one chiropodist or podiatrist is similar to the work of other chiropodists and podiatrists. Midwives are authorized only to provide services related to pregnancy.

A narrow scope of practice appears to be satisfactory when all affected professionals offer fairly similar kinds of services to patients with similar kinds of problems, as with optometrists, chiropodists and midwives.

The Minister of Health of Ontario, with the advice of the Regulated Health Professions Advisory Council, is in the process of deciding how to define the scope of practice of nurse practitioners with advanced skills. The Ontario Medical Association and the Ontario College of Physicians and Surgeons have asked that the scope of practice of nurse practitioners be described in specific terms, and that a single scope of practice apply to all nurse practitioners. They recommend, for example, that if nurse practitioners are given authority to prescribe prescription drugs, then that authority should apply only to a limited number of drugs which are identified in the regulations.

Attempting to prepare a list of drugs which nurse practitioners should be allowed to prescribe is much more difficult than producing such a list for chiropodists or optometrists. The difficulties arise from the clinical diversity of nurse practitioners. The list of drugs appropriate for, and which can be competently prescribed by, a nurse practitioner who provides only geriatric care is distinctly different from the list of drugs which can be competently prescribed by a nurse practitioner who provides primarily pediatric or mental health services.

Using only one list to describe the drugs which all specialist nurses (or even all primary care nurse practitioners) are competent to use is as difficult as trying to write a similar list for all family physicians. The list cannot include all of the drugs which can be competently used by one practitioner without listing drugs which other practitioners are not competent to use.

If all nurses, all nurse practitioners or all nurses with specialist skills are to be governed by a single scope of practice, then that scope of practice should be open-ended. It may not need to be as broad as the scope of practice of physicians, but it must be broad enough to allow different nurses to provide very different types of care and make very different types of decisions. Nurses, especially specialist nurses, will not be able to practice to their potential unless the regulations governing them have a great deal of the flexibility which exists in the regulations governing physicians.

The constraints which a narrowly defined scope of practice would place on nurses are not consistent with the flexibility offered to physicians. The constraints of a narrow scope of practice do not acknowledge the likelihood that nurses will act as professionally as do physicians. A narrow scope of practice for nurses also presumes that the College of Nurses will not be as responsible as the College of Physicians and Surgeons in fulfilling its mandate for public protection.

There is a need for either a quite open-ended description of the scope of practice of nurses (so that both generalist and specialist nurses can legally provide the full spectrum of services which they are competent to provide) or for a completely separately defined scope of practice for each kind of nurse. The open-ended model used for physicians is preferable.

Physicians in Ontario, in their recommendation that the scope of practice of nurse practitioners be narrow, are merely serving their own interests. If public safety requires that the scope of practice of each type of clinical nurse specialist be narrowly defined, then public safety requires that the same approach be used for physicians.

It would be possible to describe a separate scope of practice for each kind of physician. Separate laws, or separate sets of regulations, could specify the procedures and prescriptions considered to be within the competence of pediatricians, obstetricians, orthopedic surgeons, family physicians, etc.

The implications of changes in roles

Changes affect users, providers and payers.

As more professionals practice independently, users will have greater opportunity to go to different people and places for care.

Users may be able to find providers who are more culturally accept-able. Access to services should improve. Changes may bring greater opportunities for users to be involved in health care decisions (although the paternalism of traditional health care providers has decreased significantly in recent years).

Users may worry that increased specialization of professionals such as nurses and physiotherapists will further fragment care. Specialization brings narrowness, and as more workers become involved in the care of one patient there is a greater need for attention to coordination, information flow and communication between providers. Specialization brings more referrals and a greater need for a case manager or equivalent who will represent the interests of the user.

Changes in roles may improve quality. The ability of less-exten-sively trained personnel to work independently can be underesti-mated. When Saskatchewan, in the early 1970s, introduced its chil-dren's dental program using dental nurses (later renamed dental therapists) it was assumed that a high degree of dentist supervision would be needed. It was assumed that there would be one dentist for each three therapists. As the program developed, the use of dentists gradually decreased until there were close to 20 dental therapists on staff for every supervising dentist. The decreased dentist supervi-sion was encouraged by the studies of quality which showed that the work of the therapists was superior to that of dentists. The aban-donment of the dental therapists in the 1980s was a triumph of pol-itics over rationality, but the decade of Saskatchewan experience with a new provider of dental care illustrates the validity of testing new roles for new personnel.

Changes can, for professionals, mean altered incomes, altered employment opportunities, altered career ladders, altered relation-ships to other professionals, altered job satisfaction and a new per-sonal and professional image. Role changes could, when they lead to increased repetition, lead to less job satisfaction.

New referral patterns will develop. Physicians will need to become accustomed to referrals from, and referrals to, nurses, physiothera-pists and other professionals working as independent practitioners.

Changes in roles will often affect physician incomes. How many physicians will be affected, what types of physicians will be affect-ed and how much incomes will change is not clear. The size of the effect on physician incomes will depend on how many other pro-fessionals provide services previously provided by physicians, the range of services these other professionals will be allowed to pro-vide, whether physician's fees will be kept at their present levels, the degree to which user fees are allowed, how much money from the physician global account will be used to make payments to other professionals, the levels at which individual and collective physician payments are capped, how many physicians will have medicare billing numbers and how much the supply of physicians increases or decreases. Effects on family physicians will almost surely be different than the effects on specialists, and effects on specialists will vary from specialty to specialty.

Changes in roles will increase competition between providers. The competition will be for patients, power and/or dollars.

Multiple sources of care will decrease the inconvenience or hazard faced by users in the event of strikes or other job actions by one type of health care professional.

Summary

Many changes in the scope of practice of health care professionals have occurred. The changes have been planned and unplanned, avoidable and unavoidable. Some have been welcomed, some derided and some fought against. Some have been in the public interest and some in someone else's interest. Some of the changes have lowered costs and others have increased costs. Quality has been improved in some cases and lowered in others. Generally speaking, health care which is delivered by more than one type of provider appears to be of reasonable quality regardless of who delivers it.

To date, changes in the roles of professionals who work within the medical model have seldom occurred unless approved by physicians. Physicians have decided which services they wish to "delegate" to someone else. The delegation of functions by physicians to other professionals often has not fully acknowledged the competence of the other professionals, but the delegation which has occurred has illustrated the feasibility of transferring services from physicians to other providers.

Changes in roles can be impeded by the law. Laws can make it illegal for health care workers to discuss a diagnosis with a patient and can prevent competent professionals from ordering investigations and prescribing prescription drugs. The law can also create inequitable access to public funding. Fortunately, there have been some early moves towards correction of inequities which exist.

Legislation in all provinces except Ontario gives physicians special powers and it limits opportunities for other professionals. Traditional legislation preserves a degree of physician dominance which is not in the public interest and which is unfair to other professionals. All provinces should consider copying the concepts inherent in the Ontario Regulated Health Professions Act.

Nurses and/or other health care professionals have fully established their competency in community mental health, pain control, palliative care, rehabilitation, intensive care, dialysis, occupational health, emergency care, home care, primary health care, obstetrics, hearing loss assessment and many other fields. These competencies should be recognized in the legal scope of practice of the affected professionals.

A narrow scope of practice which applies to all nurses will seriously limit the ability of nurses, especially specialist nurses, to serve the public. Efforts by physicians to sharply limit the scope of practice of nurses is certainly in the best interest of physicians, but it is not in the best interest of taxpayers, patients, communities or nurses.

A narrow scope of practice appears to be satisfactory when all providers in a group see similar patients and deliver similar services. It is not appropriate for any profession in which the practitioners are significantly different in the skills they have and the kinds of services they are competent to provide.

Physicians, dentists and nurses are the professions whose members are most diverse in the skills they have and the patients they serve. An open-ended scope of practice is therefore most appropriate for these three professions.

Responses to suggested changes in the roles of various professionals are sometimes predictable. It was predictable that dentists would object to denturists dealing directly with the public, and that physicians would object to the emergence of midwives and nurse practitioners. These objections were, and are, based a bit in pride and history but mostly in economics. Almost any employment group (whether teachers, plumbers or health care professionals) objects to sharing its turf, power and income.

Chapter 1 has described and discussed the factors which have been, and usually still are, important to the way in which human resources are used in the delivery of health care. It has set the stage for later chapters which discuss the widening of choices for those who use health care and those who pay for it.

Chapter 1 has described the devices by which those with power and privilege, mostly physicians, have opposed change. Later chapters identify possible futures, identify and evaluate strategies, discuss the financial and patient care implications of the various strategies and suggest how altered use of health care professionals can lower the cost of health care without reducing quality.

In the future, more practitioners will function independently and more will be able to order investigations and write prescriptions. Turf wars will accelerate, as between optometrists and ophthalmologists, between primary care nurse practitioners and family physicians and between clinical nurse specialists and specialist physicians.

It is fortunate for society that the health care playing fields are being leveled. It is to be hoped that governments and consumers will encourage, and at times demand, rational, cooperative and mature communication between the various members of the health care team.

As the 20th century ends, some of the historical obstructions to sensible use of health care professionals are disappearing. The sky is the limit in terms of new patterns of health care delivery.

CHAPTER 2

The Context in Which Changes in Roles are Occurring

New roles for health care professionals will be planned and introduced better if there is a reasonable understanding of the context in which the changes will occur.

The environment of health care 30 to 40 years ago

In the 1950s and 1960s, good health care was thought to be the key to a healthy population. Physicians and hospitals were thought to be the only really important parts of health care. Everyone assumed that health care professionals, especially physicians, routinely gave good advice and made good decisions.

Health care, in particular physician care and hospital care, was thought to be worth any price. Governments attempted to fund all of the health care which physicians ordered. More doctors and hospitals were wanted and supplied. Unlimited access to publicly funded hospital and doctor care was considered to be the right of every Canadian.

Consumers had few rights. Physician decisions were seldom questioned. The decisions and actions of physicians were evaluated only by other physicians.

The 1996 environment of health care

Canadian governments are broke. Previous levels of spending on the social programs to which Canadians have become accustomed, including our publicly financed health care, can no longer be afforded.

The federal government is reducing its transfer payments to the provinces. Provinces have capped spending on health care and have capped spending in all of the major sectors within health care. Public spending on health care in Canada in 1993-94 was only 0.15% greater than in 1992-93. Total public spending on health care has significantly decreased in several provinces, and decreases will continue. The per cent of the Canadian gross national product (GNP) spent on health care has, in the last few years, fallen from 10.3% to 9.9% (Michael Rachlis, Toronto, January 1996), and the portion of this spending which is from public sources is decreasing. (Some analysts believe total spending on health care has fallen even lower than 9.9% of GNP.)

Today, there is general agreement that health care is not as important to the health status of Canadians as are personal and collective wealth, genetics, emotional support, physical environments, personal choices and public policy. The prevention of injury and ill health is now known to occur primarily in homes, workplaces, classrooms, legislatures and communities rather than in hospitals and in doctors' offices.

Health care must now compete with education, road construction, the old age pension, day care, environmental protection and other social spending for scarce public dollars. In this competition for the tax dollar, health care has lost much of its historical advantage. Health care is not as sacred as it once was. Endless public funding of health care is no longer seen as sensible. It is now acceptable to limit public spending on health care so that governments are able to allocate money to other social policy areas which also are important to health.

Consumers are now in charge. They want their priorities to be honoured, and in their priorities quality of life is as important as length of life.

Public ambivalence is rampant. Canadians as consumers want medicare preserved, including the five basic principles of universality, accessability, comprehensiveness, portability and public administration, but there is also widespread support for the principles of affordability and costeffectiveness. Canadians as consumers want unlimited free physician and hospital care, but as taxpayers they want no more taxes. The importance of community-based care and outpatient drugs is accepted, but the public also supports the Canada Health Act, which protects access to only physicians and hospitals.

Governments know they are not currently financing all useful health care, but there is still a pretence that we have, or should have, a one-tier health care system.

Many politicians and much of the public still state that user fees are unacceptable but calmly accept user fees (sometimes as much as 100% of cost) in association with outpatient drugs, chiropractic care, assistive devices, ambulances, dental care, outpatient physiotherapy, alternative therapies and eye glasses. User fees are, for reasons which are not easily seen, acceptable with respect to all services except those received from hospitals and physicians.

Waste is now the greatest threat to the preservation of publicly funded basic health care for all Canadians. There is strong evidence that at least one quarter of all professional decisions are inappropriate, but very few resources are being assigned to improving professional decisions and avoiding health care which is not cost-effective.

Expansion of the roles of specialist physicians

Fifty years ago, there were very few of the health care professionals who are accepted and necessary today. The roles of physiotherapists, medical social workers and clinical dieticians were just becoming recognized. Respiratory therapists, dental hygienists, paramedics, clinical specialist nurses, most physician specialists and most of the other 40 to 50 health care professionals who now exist were not yet being trained and often were not yet thought of.

Fifty years ago, everything was very simple. Physicians were in charge of almost all health care except that which was delivered by dentists and chiropractors. Some physicians were specialists, but family physicians continued to provide most of the services provided by specialists. Even when specialization became well established in the '50s and '60s, most family physicians continued to do surgery, give anesthetics, deliver babies and admit patients to hospital.

But almost everything changed.

Physician specialists increased their power and became more and more superspecialized. They are now the sole providers of most new procedures and techniques within their fields. They now provide almost 100% of hospital care in urban centres.

As specialization became more fully established, family physicians were gradually eased out of surgery, anesthesia, obstetrics, pathology, radiology, electrocardiography and many other types of medical care. The range of activities of family physicians became markedly different from that of specialists. (Figure 2.1) The divergence between the scope of practice of family physicians and of specialist physicians occurred partly because family physicians were restricted to a smaller range of services and partly because technology produced many new services which were delivered only by specialist physicians.

Specialization also increased in nursing, physiotherapy, occupational therapy and dentistry. Fifty years ago, the Registered Nurse (RN) was the only recognized nursing worker, and every nurse was considered competent to work in every type of nursing situation. Now there are trained nursing assistants below the RN level, and there are a variety of recognized nurse specialists. Even nurses who obtain no formal specialist training after graduation tend to work exclusively in one clinical field such as mental health, pediatrics, the emergency room or ophthalmology. Over time, nurses who graduated as generalists acquire special skills in their chosen field and they lose most of the skills they once had in other clinical fields.

The scope of practice of only a few professionals, including optometrists and chiropractors, has remained relatively unchanged.

Figure 2.1

**Changes in the Scope of Practice of
Family Physicians and Specialist Physicians - 1950 to 2000**

Volume

MD specialists

Family physicians

1950   1960   1970   1980   1990   2000

The general trend depicted in Figure 2.1 applies to all specialty fields, but the dominance of specialists is not the same in all specialties. In some fields such as pediatrics there is still significant overlap between the activities of family physicians and specialists; in other fields such as cardiovascular surgery there is very little overlap.

Sometimes many professionals are now involved in the delivery of care within one clinical field. Care of the feet, for example, may be provided by chiropodists, podiatrists, physiotherapists, nurses and chiropractors as well as family physicians and physician specialists. In obstetrics, midwives (in Ontario) now have a status roughly equivalent to that of family physicians. In mental health, the care delivery team includes social workers, psychologists, case managers, nurses, counsellors, ombudsmen and occupational therapists. Some professionals bring unique skills, but usually there is significant overlap in the areas of competence of the various professionals who work in the same clinical field.

The shaded portion of Figure 2.1 represents services and activities which are currently performed by specialist physicians but which are appropriate for delivery by less expensive personnel. This theme will be explored in later chapters.

An emphasis on cost-effectiveness

It was at one time believed that the judgment of health care professionals, especially physicians, should not be questioned. Studies have now described endless examples of professional confusion, contradiction and error. Inappropriate decisions have been found regardless of the type of health care examined and regardless of the type of health care professional involved.

Health care is rapidly moving into an era in which professional decisions will be routinely questioned and evaluated. Users and payers will examine the appropriateness of at least a significant minority of the investigations and care recommended by, or provided by, health care professionals.

In addition to concern regarding the appropriateness of professional decisions, users and payers are concerned about the cost of services. There is ample evidence that the cost of many services is higher than it should be.

Users, managers and payers increasingly demand proof that the services being provided are the appropriate ones, and proof that the appropriate services are being provided at the lowest possible cost.

The changing roles of government

All provinces have accepted the challenge of a larger role in many aspects of health care (Figure 2.2).

Figure 2.2

TheChanging Role of Provincial Governments

From	To
Insurance company	Planner, manager and funder
Financial protection of patients	Quality protection as well as financial protection
Paying for whatever the health care providers say is needed	Controlled spending; ceilings on everything;
Professional decisions unquestioned	Professional decisions monitored
Health care as a top priority	Health status as the top priority
Increasing inputs	Increasing outcomes
Health status protected by the the "Health" department	Health status protected by all gov't departments
Emphasis on doctors and hospitals	Emphasis on community care and health promotion
Support for the medical model	Abandonment of the medical model
Sickness policy	Health policy
A bureaucratic, authoritarian Ministry of Health	Partnerships with consumers and providers

(Adapted from: Spending Smarter and Spending Less, Sutherland and Fulton, 1994, p. 73.)

The role of government is changing and health care cannot control or ignore the changes.

Greater public accountability

Professions are being increasingly asked to demonstrate in an open and understandable way that consumer complaints are being dealt with. Specific problem areas such as sexual abuse are being given special attention.

Individual providers are obliged by law and ethics to provide users with a clear explanation of diagnostic and treatment options and of the implications of each of the options. Users must be given the opportunity to select the care which best suits their values, preferences and willingness to take risks.

The new demands for accountability have brought tensions and expense. Provincial Colleges of Physicians and Surgeons have increased staff and fees in response to the new demands. In Ontario in November 1994, disciplinary hearings into complaints against physicians were being booked into 1997, a schedule which reflected the sharp rise in the number of complaints and the inability of the professional bureaucracy to handle the volume. (*Dialogue*, The College of Physicians and Surgeons of Ontario, November 1994, p. 3.)

Physicians have for many years had peer review processes in place. These processes may be voluntary or they may have legal status. The Ontario Peer Assessment Program each year formally reviews a number of physicians for competence (defined as whether a physician is capable of doing the right thing) and performance (defined as whether the right thing is actually done). (Kaiga, T., "Making the Grade: The Physician Review Program", CPSO *Dialogue*, November 1994, pp. 5-8.)

Expansions in the scope of practice of professionals such as nurses will almost surely lead to greater expenditures by them on public accountability. Increased professional accountability and sensitivity will be a prerequisite to preservation of the professional independence which is wanted.

An expanding number of gatekeepers

Health care professionals do not just deliver services; they also often determine which services will be delivered, and to whom.

Control over the services which consumers will receive (the gatekeeper function) is highly prized. It brings power, prestige and, for some providers, additional income.

Early in the 20th century, dentists and allopathic physicians were the clear victors in the struggle to be the gatekeepers to health care in Canada. As the 20th century ends, however, the gatekeeping function has become more dispersed. Changes in legislation, in combination with greater appreciation of the competence of a variety of health care providers, have led to many professionals being gatekeepers in specific situations.

Public Health Nurses have had their own caseload, and have designed care plans for each person in that caseload, for decades. In these roles they act as gatekeepers.

Home care case managers, who are usually nurses but who may be social workers or other professionals, are gatekeepers. They determine the eligibility of persons for home care and determine what services these persons will receive. These case managers often largely control the extent to which physicians will be involved in care. Physicians may become involved only when the patient requires a prescription or investigation which cannot be authorized by a nurse or other provider.

Social workers, and sometimes other persons, regularly control access to halfway houses, sheltered workshops, addiction rehabilitation programs, group homes and a variety of other forms of social support.

Psychologists evaluate individuals and determine the need for special educational and counselling assistance.

Ambulance dispatchers determine the order of importance of ambulance calls. Nurses and paramedics screen persons arriving at hospital emergency departments to assure early attention to those with the most urgent needs.

Physicians still control access to most prescription drugs, but limited authority has been granted to other providers of medical care such as dentists, chiropodists, podiatrists, midwives, paramedics and optometrists. Selected nurse practitioners and clinical specialist nurses will, hopefully, soon be added to the list.

Public servants or insurance company employees, who may or may not be health care professionals, evaluate requests for admission to institutions, for eligibility for mobility and other aids, and for access to expensive drugs.

Audiologists determine whether a person requires a hearing aid, and they are the professionals most likely to determine what type of hearing aid is required. Occupational therapists often decide whether a disabled person is competent to drive a motor vehicle.

Physicians, especially specialists, have traditionally been the gatekeepers for hospital care, but some changes are occurring. Midwives can now admit in Ontario.

It is still usually physicians who refer patients for laboratory, X-ray and other investigative services, but the number of other professionals who can order or provide these services is increasing. Chiropractors have for many years offered X-ray services, and in some provinces these services are covered by the provincial medicare plans. In Ontario, licensed midwives can order laboratory and imaging (X-ray and ultrasound) services, and in 1995 the Minister of Health announced that similar opportunities would soon be available to some nurse practitioners. (As of July 1996, the Minister was still considering a recommendation from his Advisory Committee regarding nurse practitioners. The Committee recommended that these nurses be allowed to order a limited number of laboratory tests and to order ultrasound but not X-rays.)

Consumers also have gatekeeper roles. They decide when to visit an office or emergency department, and they have direct access to an increasing number of diagnostic tests. Pregnancy testing and diabetic testing are perhaps the most common of these tests, but other diagnostic kits are also available.

There is no longer any need to question the ability of many different professionals to act as gatekeepers in specific circumstances. Energies should now be applied to the question of which professionals should have this function in which situations.

There is not yet a full appreciation of the frequency with which a variety of health care professionals act as gatekeepers to health care. In describing deficiencies in our current health care system the January 1994, *Report of the Nova Scotia Task Force on Primary Health Care* stated:

> "It (the primary health care system) exclusively uses physicians as the entry point to the system, when it is recognized that many problems are of a social rather than a medical origin and people could be served as well, or better, by another care provider." (p. 23)

Only two of fourteen members of this Task Force were physicians. The fact that such a group would identify entry to health care as a physician prerogative, and would limit other health care providers to evaluating "social" problems, suggests a mind set which will obstruct rapid expansion of the gatekeeping functions of nurses and other health care professionals.

Summary

The 21st century will not be merely an extension of the 20th century. Future years will not bring more of the same. Health care and its environment will continue to change.

Many factors support less public spending on health care. The dominant factors are the financial crunch faced by all governments and the evidence that health care dollars are not spent well.

The professional lives of health care professionals are changing, and these changes will continue. Monitoring by outside agencies and governments has placed new limits on professional freedom. The incomes of physicians are increasingly controlled by governments. Patient priorities and wishes must be respected by all health care providers. Professionals face the possibility of unemployment and uncertainty of other kinds.

The changes described in this chapter have not evolved overnight. They represent a steady progression from the health care milieu of former decades to the quite different milieu which exists today.

The Policy Options

This chapter describes several policy options which are available to governments as they amend the way in which health care professionals are utilized. Variations are possible within the basic options.

In the evaluation of major policy options, special attention is given to opportunities for delivery by other professionals of services currently being delivered by specialist physicians.

Option #1 – Preserve the status quo

Provinces which keep the historical "Medical Acts" (by whatever name) will automatically be opting for the status quo. Ontario has already rejected this option.

The status quo is difficult to define when so many things are changing, but in this chapter the status quo is the medical hierarchical health care model which still exists in most provinces.

If the status quo is preserved, physicians will remain the dominant medical care professionals. They will remain the only professionals authorized to provide most medical care, and they will retain a high degree of control over the range of functions which can legally be provided by professionals such as nurses, laboratory technologists, X-ray technologists, physiotherapists, occupational therapists, respiratory therapists and ambulance attendants.

Retaining the medical model with its hierarchy (with physicians at the top of the hierarchy) does not mean there can be no changes in the duties of professionals who are lower on the totem pole. It does mean that changes will be largely dependent on the decisions of physicians. Changes in roles will usually occur only when physicians delegate new duties to other providers.

Retaining the medical model need not prevent other changes in the health care system from occurring. Cost control can continue, although it will be made more difficult by the inability to transfer functions to less-expensive personnel. Provinces will continue to be able to reduce expenditures on physician's services by lowering the ceilings on total physician payments, on payments to specific specialty groups and/or on individual physician payments. Provinces will continue to be able to lower the fees paid to physicians, but experience has shown that simply lowering physician fees does not reduce total payments to physicians. If total costs are to fall, lower fees must be combined with lower physician payment ceilings. Retaining the medical model also need not prevent reductions in the number of physicians able to bill medicare.

Whether or not the medical model is preserved, provinces could also implement programs to reduce the volume of health care which is not cost-effective. This will protect the incomes of those providers, especially physicians, who have been careful in their clinical decisions. It will put pressure on those who have been delivering inappropriate care. (The options for lowering costs and improving spending are discussed in detail in *Spending Smarter and Spending Less*, Sutherland and Fulton, 1994.)

Preservation of the status quo will prevent optimal use of other professionals. It will interfere with experimentation with new types of training and specialization. It will interfere with wise spending. It will make it more difficult for governments to promote expanded roles for midwives, psychologists, clinical nurse specialists and others. There will be continued expansion of the roles of physician specialists and continued payments to specialists for many services which could be delivered by others at lower cost.

The status quo is seen by some as culturally unsatisfactory. In maternity care and women's health care, for example, consumers have asked for something other than the paternalistic and male-dominated medical model. (The desired changes may not require professional substitution. Some consumers will be content if services are delivered by female rather than male physicians.)

Preserving the status quo will increase the frustrations of those professionals whose scope of practice is largely determined by physicians.

Legislated changes in Ontario have made preservation of the traditional status quo even more unacceptable in other provinces than it previously was. Political pressure for change in other provinces will inevitably grow as nurses, physiotherapists, etc., seek greater career opportunities.

The status quo has strengths as well as weaknesses.

The greatest strength of the status quo is that it exists. Change is difficult and it usually carries risks. Both politicians and bureaucrats may wish to avoid the hassles and hazards of change. The status quo can be quite unattractive and still be seen as better than the struggles associated with implementing something new.

Preservation of the status quo reduces pressures on educational institutions. They will not face the challenges inherent in training/educating new types of health care professionals or assisting existing professionals to develop new skills. There will be minimal pressure to create new specialist programs for nurses and others because there will be only very limited opportunities for these specialists to use their skills.

If the current rights and powers of physicians are maintained, there will be less need to continue to reduce medical school enrolment.

The status quo is made attractive by the lack of aggressive public demand for major changes in the roles of health care providers, although public attitudes could change if the public becomes aware of the benefits of changes in roles.

If the status quo is maintained, governments do not have to face the problems associated with transfer of physician functions to other professionals. These problems include confrontations between governments and physicians, confrontations between different professionals, the need for new legislation and the need to explain the changes to the public.

The status quo has other more hidden attractions. If the roles of other professionals are expanded, public expenditures on physician services will fall. Some, and perhaps many, physicians will not have a provincial billing number. Physicians who are unable to bill medicare will either work within a private health care system, be unemployed or move to some other country, and these possibilities are politically unattractive.

The presence of physicians who cannot work within the public system would almost surely lead to an expansion of privately financed health care. Some provinces do not wish this expansion. If expanding the roles of nurses and other health care professionals accelerates the development of private health care services, then the expansion may not be attractive to some provinces.

Option #2 – Promote new types of health care providers

Many completely new health care professionals and paraprofessionals have joined the health care team in the last 60 years. Examples include respiratory therapists, speech language pathologists, audiologists, optical technicians, occupational therapists, cytology technicians, denturists, athletic therapists, dental technicians, dental hygienists and massage therapists. Each of these providers has a separate educational program, title and area of expertise. Each appeared because there were services which needed to be provided and existing professionals could not provide them and/or did not want to provide them.

It is difficult to know when to create another separate health care provider rather than increase the skills of an established profession, but at times the option of a new type of provider will be chosen.

Ontario had options when, in 1994, it legitimized midwifery and approved the establishment of midwife training programs. It could have recognized only nurse midwives, only nonnurse midwives, or both. It could have established training programs for nurse midwives, nonnurse midwives, or both. The province chose to establish new undergraduate programs which would graduate a nonnurse midwife. Midwives will be trained in new four-year programs in three Ontario universities. Nurse midwives who graduated elsewhere are able to practice in Ontario if approved standards are met, but programs for the training of nurse midwives have not been approved.

The approval of new professionals may increase the likelihood of turf wars and of poor understanding of the roles of other professionals, but this is only conjecture. There is little evidence pertaining to the question of the extent to which teamwork, or lack of it, is related to the way in which providers are educated. It does appear, however, that expanding the skills of an existing professional will often cost less than creating a new provider.

A variety of completely new health care providers could be produced (Figure 3.1).

Figure 3.1

Possibilities for New Professionals

Genetic technicians	Genetic advisors
Endoscopists	Mental health therapists
Dermatology therapists	Skin care technologists
Gynecology therapists	Dialysis specialists
Diabetic therapists	Orthopedic therapists
Gastroenterology therapists	Pediatric therapists
Primary care geriatric therapists	Neonatal intensive care specialists
Occupational health specialists	

New types of health care providers may supplement, work for, replace, or compete with, physicians, nurses or other professionals. For example, competition between nurses and dialysis technicians trained on the job is already present, as is competition between nurse midwives and midwives who are not also nurses.

New health care providers may or may not provide services which were formerly provided exclusively by physicians or dentists. If new independent health care providers provide services which were formerly provided only by physicians or dentists, the new professionals may need the protection of special legislation such as was used to allow optometrists and chiropractors to practice outside of physician control.

Option #3 – Expand the functions of existing professionals (other than physicians)

There is ample evidence that nurses and other professionals could, usually with additional training, provide many services which they are not presently allowed to provide.

Rapid expansion of the scope of practice of nurses, and of other professionals who are within the medical model, can occur only by expansion into areas of service which are currently the domain of physicians. This being the case, expansions will seldom occur if they must be approved by physicians.

Expansions in the range of services offered by nurses, respiratory technologists, physiotherapists, etc., can, when the traditional powers of physicians are in place, occur in three ways. First, "medical" services can be delegated by physicians to other professionals. Second, new services not considered to be "medical" services can be performed without physician approval. For nurses, for example, this second category of services includes anything designated a "nursing" service, e.g., the services provided by nurses with special skills in operating rooms, intensive care units, infection control, geriatric care, community nursing, occupational health, etc. Services which fall into the second category can be performed without delegation from a physician. Third, professionals may expand their scope of practice by obtaining the protection of a special statute.

Expanding the scope of practice (the authorized functions) of nurses and other professionals becomes much easier when authority for change rests with the Minister of Health rather than with physicians.

Expanded roles for nurses are examined in greater detail in Chapter 4. Expanded roles for other professionals are examined in Chapter 5.

Professionals who obtained independent status through passage of a special statute can seek an expanded scope of practice through amendments to their statutes.

Option #4 – Convert family physicians into minispecialists

Efforts to move family physicians into service areas now served primarily or exclusively by specialists would represent a significant change in policy, but this option may become attractive if nurses indicate they do not wish to provide services currently being provided by specialist physicians.

There is an oversupply of family physicians. Many feel threatened by the appearance of new primary care professionals, by decreasing provincial spending on physician's services, by the possibility of limits on billing numbers, by increased monitoring and regulation of their clinical decisions and by competition from physician specialists.

Many family physicians would welcome the income security, job security and job satisfaction which would come from being allowed to deliver services currently being provided by specialists in anesthesia, surgery, psychiatry, pediatrics, geriatrics, oncology, etc.

Expanded roles for family physicians is a viable policy option, although not the best option. There are no legal impediments. There will be few if any user objections. Technical quality will be easily assured. There would be few educational/training problems. The reductions which have occurred in specialty training programs has left considerable educational space in the teaching hospitals. The only significant obstacle will be the opposition of physician specialists.

Minispecialization is common in group practices comprised primarily or entirely of family physicians. Usually all family physicians in the group provide a broad range of medical services, but many also have special expertise in one clinical field such as obstetrics, anesthesia, surgery or pediatrics. The amount of training that is required to give a family physician the competence to perform a significant part of the services currently being provided by orthopedic surgeons, psychiatrists, allergists, etc., is unclear, but one year or less has historically been considered adequate.

The development of minispecialists is more feasible now that most provinces require an MD graduate to have three years of residency experience before he/she can be licensed for independent practice.

Specialists could attempt to prevent the granting of hospital privileges to minispecialists. Specialists could also refuse to participate in shortened specialty training programs. Specialist obstructions should, however, if they emerge, be able to be overcome by governments who combine firmness with a willingness to be flexible.

Minispecialist family physicians need not have any special professional designation, although it is likely that some form of identification would emerge.

Expanded use of family physicians as minispecialists will not be attractive to payers if it leads to higher total expenditures on physician services. If this option is to be attractive to Ministries of Health, payments to specialists must go down at least enough to compensate for additional payments to family physicians.

Summary

Governments who wish to reduce costs by transfer of functions to less expensive providers should examine the policy options described in Chapter 3. The options which may lead to lower human resource costs are the introduction of new professionals, the expansion of the functions of family physicians and the expansion of the scope of practice of other existing professionals.

The human resource policy options which have been described in Chapter 3 are not mutually exclusive. Any province can preserve the status quo in some parts of health care, expand the roles of existing professionals in other parts of health care and create new workers to provide services in other parts of health care.

The idea of expanded roles for a variety of health care providers is not new, but the emphasis has usually been on expanded roles in the provision of primary care (Shugars, D., O'Neil, E. and Bader J., *Healthy America: Practitioners for 2005*, The Pew Health Professions Commission, 1991; *Starting Points*, a government report in Alberta in 1993; WHO documents). Few sources have recommended significant expansion in the use of other professionals to provide services which are now provided by specialist physicians, although the idea is not totally new.

> "For at least 20 years there has been a growing interest in the possibility of using "intermediate level health practitioners"... to perform... functions currently performed by physicians, dentists and pharmacists. An extensive literature, based in part on experimental and field experience, has developed which demonstrates the technical feasibility

of such substitution over a wide range of functions, while maintaining quality standards equal to or better than those achieved by the "peak professionals"." (Evans, R.G., *Strained Mercy*, Butterworths, 1984, p. 143.)

Most services can be delivered satisfactorily by more than one type of professional, and good policy selection will increase the likelihood that the preferred professional will be the least expensive one who can deliver care of the desired quality. Whichever professional is used, that professional should not be expected to always make the right decisions.

Two of the policy options described encourage use of the health care provider who can deliver the desired quality of care at the lowest cost. Only one of the policy options, retaining the status quo with its emphasis on specialist care, will not lead to use of lower-cost providers.

The general objective of using the lowest-cost provider who can deliver services of good quality is simple, but accomplishing this objective is not. There will be many disagreements over quality, and great resistance from providers who see "their" services being delivered by others. The controversies which will be associated with change should not, however, prevent acceptance of the idea that new roles for many providers are possible and desirable.

CHAPTER 4

Expanded Roles for Nurses

"Often called a sleeping giant, the nursing profession in Canada is awakening to the unique skills and insights it contributes to the delivery of health services and the quest for an economically sustainable health care future."

This observation was made by Baumgart and Larsen, in their book *Canadian Nurses Face the Future* (p. 3). The same authors suggest that the future of nursing should represent a balance of knowledge, tasks, ethics, psychological needs, economic rewards and politics.

This chapter examines policies and actions which may more completely awaken the "sleeping giant", while enhancing the suggested balance. It discusses options available to nurses who wish expanded roles. It discusses factors which are impeding the progress of nurses towards expanded roles as well as factors which are a source of optimism.

The statistical dominance of nurses

One of the sources of optimism is the statistical dominance of nurses. Their numbers make them a key to the future of health care (Table 4.1).

Nursing personnel represent over half of all professional health care providers. The number of nurse graduates every year (diploma and baccalaureate) is about five times the number of physician graduates. There are four nurses for every physician in Canada, and one practising registered nurse for every 125 Canadians. Total enrollment in nursing programs has fallen in recent years, but the percentage drop appears to have been no greater than the drop in enrollment in medical schools (from 28,001 in 1990 to 26,993 in 1994) (Canadian Nurses Association). The reduction is related to the increasing emphasis on a baccalaureate qualification.

When considering the transfer of functions from physicians to nurses, it may be useful to be aware of the number of physicians in the various categories. Eight types of physicians represent over 80% of all physicians (Tables 4.2 and 4.3.).

Table 4.1

Numbers of health care professionals in Canada, 1986+		
Audiologists	2,660	
Chiropractors	2,913	
Dieticians	4,664	
Laboratory technologists	16,875	
Occupational Therapists	2,463	
Opticians	3,200	
Optometrists	2,386	
Pharmacists	16,209	
Physicians	51,966	
Physiotherapists	5,729	11,000 (1990)*
Radiology technologists	10,339	
Registered Nurses	219,000	265,000 (1994)**
Registered Social Workers	9,323	
Respiratory technologists	2,766	

+ *Health Personnel in Canada*, Health Canada, 1988.
* *A Vision for Physiotherapy Service Delivery*, The Canadian Physiotherapy Association, 1992.
** Canadian Nurses Association, 1994.

Table 4.2

The Dominant Physician Types	
Family physicians	47.8%
Surgeons (all types)	9.3%
Psychiatrists	5.7%
Anesthetists	4.6%
Internists	4.3%
Obstetricians/gynecologists	3.9%
Radiologists	3.9%
Pediatricians	3.4%

Winter, R.W., Editors page, *Society of Obstetricians and Gynecologists of Canada Bulletin*, July/August 1986.

Table 4.3

The Supply of Physician Specialists, Canada, 1996*

Anesthesia	1967	Dermatology	454
Diagnostic Radiology	1650	Emergency Medicine	275
Gastroenterology	262	General Surgery	2622
Immunology and allergy	68	Nephrology	140
Obstetrics and Gynecology	1617	Oncology (medical)	149
Oncology (radiation)	287	Ophthalmology	1016
Orthopedic Surgery	1011	Otolaryngology	579
Pediatrics	2018	Physical Med and Rehab	294
Psychiatry	3194	Respiratory Medicine	307
Rheumatology	223	Urology	575

*Royal College of Physicians and Surgeons. February 1996.

Because there are so many nurses, altering the roles of even a few of them could substantially change the way health care is delivered.

Using the information in Tables 4.1 and 4.3, it is clear that there are about 4000 nurses for every allergist, 260 for every orthopedic surgeon, etc. If one out of every 1000 nurses (0.1%, or 270 nurses in all of Canada) acquire special skills in the field of allergy, the number of specialist allergy nurses will be four times the total number of physician allergists. If two out of each 1000 nurses acquires special skills in orthopedic surgery, there would be half as many orthopedic nurse specialists as there are orthopedic surgeons.

A very small number of nurses with special skills plus professional independence could significantly affect the delivery of physician specialist services. These specialist nurses would alter the professional lives of physician specialists. They also could lower the cost of many services presently paid for at specialist physician rates.

About half of all physicians are specialists and half family physicians. If 5% of nurses acquire specialist status and also acquire the rights and opportunities of independent practitioners, and if they provide services formerly provided by specialist physicians, the 5% of nurses could substitute for up to 40% of all specialist physicians. If 5% of all nurses (about 14,000) begin to provide primary care, this 5% could replace up to 40% of the family physicians.

The large supply of nurses, combined with the breadth of their general and special skills, makes them unique. If the roles of even 10% of nurses expand significantly, the entire health care system will change. By comparison, changes in the roles of other health care professionals will have limited effect. Altered roles for optometrists, for example, could have a major impact on ophthalmologists but not on anyone else. Optometrist services overlap very little with the services of anyone but ophthalmologists. Similarly, X-ray technicians outnumber diagnostic radiologists about 6:1 and substitution could quickly occur if approved, but the substitution will have little effect on anyone but the diagnostic radiologists.

Factors affecting the future of nurses

The forces and factors which are shaping the future of nursing are internal and external. They are local, provincial, national and international. They are attitudinal, organizational, legal, financial and professional. They arise from history, from politics, from economics and from nurses themselves.

Internal factors include the objectives chosen by nurses, the culture of nursing (including assumptions made consciously or unconsciously), the funds available to nursing associations, how those funds are spent and the skill with which nurses use their power. External forces include the power and wealth of other health care professions, the skill with which the other professions use their power and wealth, the priorities and preferences of the public (as patients, advocates, voters and taxpayers), the general economic climate and the priorities of governments.

The goals and objectives of nurses should be clear and realistic. They should be consistent with the career expectations and preferences of most nursing students and nursing graduates. They should offer new graduates and working nurses more opportunities for specialization than now exist.

When selecting objectives it will often not be possible or desirable to seek common objectives for all nurses. Nurses by specialty and region, and as individuals, will choose different directions. The general objectives and goals of nursing should be sufficiently flexible to encompass most regional, specialty and individual preferences. Possible objectives are listed in Figure 4.1.

All of the listed objectives cannot be chosen; some are incompatible with others. The list is offered only to encourage nurses to identify and prioritize their objectives. Only then can strategies be rationally chosen and resources strategically allocated.

Many questions deserve attention as nurses and their leaders clarify their objectives.

Will nurses emphasize consolidation and protection of traditional roles or seek expanded and new roles? Will they endorse the need for specialization? Will they accept the inevitability of major conflict

Figure 4.1

Possible Objectives for Nurses

- to be identified as the primary point of entry for health care
- to be the leaders of health care delivery teams
- to promote collaborative health care delivery models
- to give consumers more choices
- to act on the political, economic, environmental and other determinants of health
- to be the primary educators of users and communities regarding health promotion
- to be assured that all future registered nurse graduates have baccalaureate degrees
- to offer nurses greater opportunity to specialize
- to assure independent practitioner status
    - for those who have acceptable qualifications
    - for those practising in the community
- to obtain the ability to prescribe prescription drugs
    - for those who have acquired appropriate skills
    - for those practising in the community
    - for those identified as specialists
- to increase nurse incomes
- to obtain payment by fee-for-service for those who choose to work as independent practitioners
- to expand the definition of "nursing"
- to avoid the delivery of "medical care" by nurses
- to compete with physicians on a level playing field
- to avoid competition with physicians
- to increase job security
- to increase gender equity
- to prevent transfer of current nursing duties to other health care workers
- to protect nurses from evaluation by non-nurses
- to reduce stress in the workplace
- to increase opportunities for career advancement
- to improve professional status
- to increase the role of nurses as patient advocates
- to have a common set of objectives for all nurses
- to allow different types of nurses to set their own objectives
- to protect the principles of medicare
- to have greater influence over health care policy
- to have greater influence over the spending of operating budgets
- to be certain that funds being spent on nursing services are being spent cost-effectively
- to be assured that nursing administrators are nurses

with physicians if there are to be major expansions in nurse roles? Will they accept, and capitalize on, the inevitability of major differences in the ways and speed with which different provinces promote or accept expanded roles for nurses? Will they appreciate their current weaknesses in the fields of policy evaluation, lobbying, consensus building and the formation of alliances? Will nurses and their leaders concentrate on the preservation of the generic nurse or grasp the opportunities which exist for new careers in specialist fields? Will they remain anxious to define "nursing care" and preserve it for nurses, or will they appreciate that nurses can deliver a very broad spectrum of care and it doesn't matter whether or not that care is called "nursing care", "medical care" or any other particular type of care?

In an American Nurses Association survey in 1993, 70% of nurses said they would take more training if they could work as independent practitioners. Nurses in Canada would probably say the same thing.

The vocabulary used by some nurses interferes with the evolution of the new roles which many nurse graduates would like to pursue. The mandate of the 1994 Alberta Task Force on Direct Access to Services Provided by Registered Nurses was: "to examine scenarios in which increased direct access to services provided by registered nurses could be implemented within health care reform." The goal of the Task Force was described as follows:

> "That the full range of nursing services be recognized and integrated as part of basic health care services in Alberta so that the public can choose to go to a registered nurse for nursing services." (*AARN Newsletter*, July/August 1994.)

Use of the term "nursing services" at the end of the preceding quote, rather than "health care", makes it difficult for the Task Force to fulfil its mandate. Nurses can define "nursing services" in any fanciful way they wish; the public will agree with physicians who will continue to define nursing services in terms of historical activities. If nurses wish to be first line providers of significant new volumes of health care, they need to see "health care" as their domain, not just "nursing services".

It would have been so much better if the goal of the Task Force had been written differently:

"That the full range of existing and potential nursing competencies be recognized and utilized in the
delivery of health care services in Alberta so that
the public can choose to go to a registered nurse for
health care."

There are strategies which can accomplish this goal, whereas
expanding the definition of "nursing services" to include everything
which some nurses will wish to do may be impossible. Expansion
of the scope of practice of nurses should not be encumbered by
semantic struggles.

The strategies chosen by provincial associations affect the future
of nurses. The nursing clinic established in Comox, B.C., in 1994,
and the nursing clinics promoted in Alberta in 1994, are designed to
promote nurses as independent providers of primary care.
Unfortunately, it is difficult or impossible to offer a reasonable
range of first-contact primary care without the authority and competence to order laboratory and other investigations, establish diagnoses, discuss care plans with patients, prescribe prescription medications and perform a broad range of therapeutic procedures.

Nurses appear to have failed to note the importance assigned by
consumers to the treatment function. They may have also overesti-
mated the ability of most nurses to adequately perform this treatment function. These failures may have contributed to the selection
of strategies which are not working.

Nursing has given considerable attention to primary care clinics
staffed by generalist nurses and operating in isolated communities.
These clinics do not contribute much to the evolution of nurse roles.
Nurses should concentrate on demonstrating their ability to serve urban
populations who have good access to physician services. Physicians
will quite happily continue to let nurses prove their ability to provide
care in isolated communities which are not attractive to physicians.

The future of nursing will be affected by the skill with which
nurses affect policy formulation. Nurses should become more adept
in their use of both the extra-parliamentary and the parliamentary
processes. In goal-setting and in the selection of strategies, there is
a need for sensitivity to the agendas and needs of governments,
communities, other professionals and individual users.

The skill with which nurses identify their sources of power and
learn how to use their power will affect the future, as will the extent
to which nurses form alliances with consumers and with other health
care providers. Networking and alliance building increase power, and
power well used increases the likelihood of a future that pleases.

The future will partly depend on the willingness of nurses to compete for dollars, for power and for patients. Part of the willingness to compete will relate to a willingness to spend. Being successful in the worlds of policy influence, labour relations, legal confrontations, proof of cost-effectiveness and public information can be expensive, and other players (in particular physicians) long ago decided to spend freely.

A wish to be cautious and loved will lead to a different future than a willingness to be aggressive in pursuing goals. A willingness to be assertive and be risk-takers will lead to a different future than a tendency to hope that someone else will lead the health care system to the changes which nurses desire.

Nursing reports have, at times, shown a strong leaning towards risk avoidance.

> "The work of nurses is extensive and overlaps with the practice of other professionals. The intent to expand the work of nurses is not an intent to extend their work beyond its professional boundaries into the practice of other disciplines." (*Challenges for Change in Health Care: Nursing in Nova Scotia*, Vol. 1, The Summary Report, Nova Scotia Task Force on Nursing, 1993.)

The first sentence is fine. The second is pussy-footing to the point of being incomprehensible. It is even more incomprehensible when read in conjunction with parts of a companion report. Volume Two of *Challenges for Change in Health Care* (*The Nova Scotia Task Force Education Subcommittee Report*, p. 48). states: "Many employers of nurses in Nova Scotia are currently investigating the impact of the expanded role of the nurse. Nurses are considered well suited to an expanded role that incorporates traditional physician practices..."

"Overlap" and expansion into "traditional physician practice" infer a potential for conflict. The greater the overlap and expansion, the greater the potential for conflict. In the presence of resource shortages the potential for conflict becomes real.

Nurses must accept the inevitability of conflict. If this is not done, nurses will be almost nonplayers as health care is reformed. Nurses must decide to either sit on the fence (and rely on consumers and payers to bring about changes which expand the roles of nurses) or to assertively seek expanded roles and struggle with the conflicts which arise.

Conflict is part of the real world. The only way to avoid it is to concede the battlefields to others who are prepared to struggle for what is in their interest.

In 1991, the Alberta College of Physicians and Surgeons forced a physician group practice in Fort McMurray to release a nurse practitioner who was working as an independent practitioner in the clinic. The nurse had a nurse practitioner certificate from the University of Alberta and a master's degree in Health Sciences. Was the prosecution of the nurse by the Alberta College of Physicians and Surgeons because the provincial medicare plan was being billed for her services or was the College also objecting to her independent practice?

At the same time as the Alberta nurse practitioner was being prosecuted, nurse practitioners practising in community health centres in Ontario and elsewhere continued to work as independent practitioners. Why are nurse practitioners in Ontario more acceptable than the nurse practitioner in Fort McMurray? One reason is that the nurse practitioner in Alberta was being paid from the global physician payment fund. Physicians see this fund as exclusively for them. In Ontario, the community health centre budgets do not affect the global funds from which physicians are paid. Payments to nurse practitioners in CHCs do not reduce the pool of money available to physicians.

The battleground is not qualifications, not public benefit and not the cost-effectiveness of health care; it is money.

Some nurses are concerned that changes in roles will lead to replacement of the current nursing emphasis on caring with an emphasis on curing. It would be helpful if nurses accepted the legitimacy of both. Caring and curing are not mutually exclusive. In some situations, technology and curing routinely overshadow caring, as in the operating room and often in an intensive care unit. In other situations, such as palliative care or community support, caring may be most central. In many situations, both caring and curing are important.

As nurses assume more responsibility in a broad spectrum of clinical situations, they will inevitably become more concerned with treatment, but additional responsibilities need not reduce attention to caring. Many physicians care deeply for their patients, and the patients of those physicians can feel the warmth and interest of their doctor. Nurses can, if they wish, continue to be caring while also delivering appropriate curative health care. The fact that some health care has been delivered by some physicians in ways which do not coincide with the perceptions of some nurses does not diminish the inherent value of curative services.

Changes in provincial laws will often be a prerequisite to significant expansion of the roles of nurses. The rapidity with which provinces revise their statutes to allow the advanced skills of specialist nurses to be used will often be as important as the acquisition of new skills. Without legislative changes, the acquisition of advanced skills may not bring the opportunity to use them, e.g., nurse practitioners are still underutilized in most provinces.

It is difficult to know whether income expectations will impede the development of new roles for nurses. If nurses seek new roles in the hope that they will approximate the incomes of the physicians now performing these roles, then few governments will be interested in change. Governments are broke, and they must be concerned about cost. If nurses seek a broader scope of practice primarily for the purposes of greater job satisfaction, more opportunities for career advancement, access to a broader range of careers and greater job security then financial considerations will be on their side. Sensitivity to fiscal constraints will strengthen the ability of nurses to accomplish their non-financial goals.

The importance of assumptions and attitudes

As discussed earlier, the goals and objectives that nurses choose, and the strategies and tactics chosen to pursue those goals and objectives, will affect the future of nursing. In turn, the attitudes and assumptions of nurses will affect the goals, objectives, strategies and tactics which nurses will choose.

Will nurses assume that health care budgets will expand to finance new roles for nurses? If so, they are naive.

Will nurses assume that their present roles in public health, community care, hospital care, health promotion and occupational health are secure, or will they assume they should take steps to protect these roles?

Will nurses assume that the public understands the importance of nurses, and that the public will come to their assistance when support is needed, or will nurses more actively seek to increase public support? Will nurses assume that they know which services are indicated in specific situations, or will they accept the need to actively examine the appropriateness of nurse decisions? Will nurses believe they already accept and protect the rights of users, or will they work with users to see how user priorities and preferences can be more fully honoured by nurses?

Will nurses take the position that their services are too important to need defending? Will nurses pretend there are Marquis of

Queensbury rules of resource allocation, or will they accept the fact that competing for resources is a never-ending and almost unsupervised form of bloodless combat?

Nursing faculty, students, practitioners and association representatives have strong, diverse and not always easily understandable opinions. All but one of the following comments come from nurses who have, or have had, leadership roles in nursing. (One comment is from a graduating nursing student.)

"You shouldn't use the term nurse practitioner; we are all just nurses."

"The family physician should cease to exist in favour of nurse practitioners."

"Nurses always lose when they disagree with physicians."

"Nurses do not want to be mini-physicians."

"Nurses do not want to compete with physicians."

"Nurses do not want to be like physicians."

"Most of what physicians do is nursing care."

"Nurses do not want to deliver medical care."

"What you are suggesting is the transfer to nurses of menial tasks currently being performed by physicians."

"Nurses are already working on pretty well everything you talk about."

The attitudes and sensitivities of some nurses are among the obstacles to change. Acquiring expanded roles is more difficult when the perceptions of nurses are negative, defensive, conflicting and/or unrealistic.

Nurses have endless amounts of ambivalence. They are divided on the issue of the legitimacy of "medical care" and of technological medicine. They are ambivalent regarding the importance of advanced skills versus advanced degrees. They still cherish the concept that all nurses are equal, a concept which is incompatible with the extent to which nurses differ in goals, powers, expectations, independence, income and emphasis.

There can be no doubt about the wish of many nurses to assume new roles in health care decisions, delivery and leadership. It is hoped that the search for new roles will not be constrained by out-of-date perceptions and attitudes.

From "the definition of nursing" to "expanded roles for nurses"

The definition of "nursing" has been the subject of numerous articles and studies. It has been a lifelong preoccupation of more than one nursing leader and academic. It has led to some definitions which are too general to be useful and which are quite different from the way the man on the street might define "nursing". Serious departure from the manner in which the term is usually used does not contribute to the evolution of the roles which nurses play.

It appears that the term "nursing services" is at times considered to be synonymous with "the scope of practice of nurses". To some, everything that is to be done by a nurse must be called "nursing". To others, all forms of health care are to be encompassed within the term "nursing". The Ontario Nursing Act, 1991, (proclaimed January 1, 1994) defines the practice of nursing as: "the promotion of health and the assessment of, the provision of care for and the treatment of health conditions by supportive, preventive, therapeutic, palliative and rehabilitative means in order to attain or maintain optimal function." It is difficult to think of any health care activity which is outside of that definition.

It may be difficult to convince the public and the legislators that suturing a wound, writing a prescription, evaluating the eligibility of a patient for publicly financed health care, delivering a baby, administering a general anesthetic, reading an electrocardiogram or providing sexual counselling are all nursing care; but all of these are things which some nurses currently do and which an increasing number of nurses should do. Is it useful to argue about whether these services are, or are not, nursing? Why has the definition of "nursing" been seen to be so important?

The answer is simple. The question of whether a service is "nursing care" versus "medical care" matters a great deal when physicians control who can provide "medical care" and nurses can only be in control of "nursing care". The same question matters very little when there are mechanisms through which nurses can be authorized to provide a broad range of health care (including all or some of "medical care") without physician agreement.

Under traditional legislation, medical acts can only be performed by physicians, by those to whom the acts are delegated by physicians, or by those protected by a special statute (as with chiropractors and optometrists). If an activity can be identified as a part of nursing, then nurses can do it without physician approval; if it is defined as a "medical" act, then nurses can perform it only with physician approval.

In those provinces in which physicians still decide the extent to which "medical" services will be provided by nurses (and other professionals within the medical model), nurses (and others) have limited likelihood of major new roles. When the scope of practice of nurses is largely determined by physicians, then the nurses have good reason to wish to expand the range of services which are called "nursing".

But the traditional legal model is on its way out. (It is already gone in Ontario.) There is now a statutory model which makes it possible for the scope of practice of nurses to expand without the approval of physicians. This new statutory model is truly a cause for optimism. (See the earlier discussion of the Ontario Regulated Health Professions Act.)

Some recent nursing reports, such as the *Nursing Service and Resource Management Plan* by the New Brunswick Department of Health and Community Services, December 1993, offer a rationale for concentrating on the future of nursing rather than the definition of it. The New Brunswick report describes the overlapping of the areas of competence of nurses and physicians. It invites emphasis on the areas of overlap.

The extent to which the roles of nurses expand will be determined largely by the size of the area of overlap. Services within the area of overlap may or may not be able to be called "nursing", but whether they are called "nursing" does not matter. What matters is the size of the area of overlap. More of the work world of the physician needs to also be within the scope of practice of nurses.

The boundaries of nursing no longer need to be defined. Energy no longer needs to be spent creating devices to circumvent anachronistic obstacles based in yesterday's status quo. Energy should now be spent on expanding the legal scope of practice of nurses rather than on defining nursing.

Nurses should put pressure on their provincial governments to introduce the type of legislation put in place in Ontario. Once the principles of the Ontario legislation are in place, nurses can then concentrate on convincing Ministers of Health that it is in the public's interest to expand the roles of nurses.

A third basis for optimism (the first two being the size of the nurse population and the availability of a new type of legislation) is the progress which nurses have already made towards expanded roles. The examples are there for everyone to see. They exist in primary, secondary and tertiary care and in health promotion and disease prevention. Many of these examples are described throughout this book.

Nurse roles in primary care

The nursing literature and the comments of many nurses indicate that primary care and health promotion are seen as the target areas for expansion of nurse roles.

This generally supported emphasis on primary care seldom is very adventurous. Many health care reports propose only very limited roles for nurses in primary care. The growth being sought is often fully within the existing scope of practice of nurses.

> "In their capacity as providers of primary health care, nurses could serve an important role in community health services, not so much by replacing medical care but by encouraging self-reliance in the community, through both formal and informal health and social support programs. They could also screen and route individuals, which might help lower the inappropriate use of other health professionals."
> (The Report of the Nova Scotia Royal Commission on Health Care, December 1989, p. 48.)

The Nova Scotia report and many other reports, including some nursing reports, offer little encouragement to nurses who wish to expand into service areas which are currently available only to physicians. Such reports are also of little help to governments who wish to deliver health care in less expensive ways. The nature of these reports is understandable when they are written by physician-dominated groups, but not when authored by nurses or others. These reports are pleasant reading only for physicians.

The Nova Scotia report did not deal with the question of how expanded roles for nurses would be funded. In the face of shrinking provincial spending on health care, no report is credible if it proposes expanded roles for nurses but fails to explain how the expanded roles will be funded. Nursing roles in primary care (and other types of care) are unlikely to grow significantly unless funded with money currently paid to physicians, and those who propose reforms to the way health care is delivered should be prepared to discuss this thorny issue.

Nursing reports quite properly recommend that nurses become more involved in disease prevention and health promotion. The health status of Canadians is likely to be protected and improved more by disease prevention and health promotion than by improvements in health care.

But nurses should also seek expanded roles in the delivery of health care. Many nurses will prefer expanded roles in diagnosis, therapy and rehabilitation, and their wishes are also legitimate. Their wishes may also be more in tune with the wishes and needs of those who fund health care.

A wish for expanded roles for nurses in the delivery of diagnostic, therapeutic and rehabilitative health care at all levels does not interfere in any way with the wish for a greater role for nurses in health promotion. There is a need for expanded roles for nurses throughout health care.

In many Health Maintenance Organizations in the United States, and in many community health centres in Canada, the first contact of a client may be with a nurse (who may or may not be a nurse practitioner). Besides being intake personnel, nurse practitioners and other nurses have their own caseload of patients who they see as required for a variety of problems. Physicians are involved in the care of these patients only if involvement is asked for by the nurse or the patient. User satisfaction is high and quality of care is comparable to that of primary care physicians.

The effectiveness of nurse practitioners and other nurses in Canada will be even greater when they are (possibly after additional training) able to prescribe prescription medication, refer to specialists and order laboratory and other investigations.

> "Legal and traditional practice restrictions, which disallow nurses from serving as primary care providers to the elderly, the worried well, and numerous other populations where the fit of knowledge and skill to need is excellent, must be viewed as unethical." (Storch, J., "Division of Labour in Health Care: Pragmatics and Ethics", in *Health, Illness and Health Care in Canada*, Second edition, 1994, pp. 543-552.)

Ontario, in late 1994, announced that nurse practitioners who met specified criteria would, in 1995, be granted authority to practice independently. They would offer general medical care, prescribe prescription medication and order investigations. (The 1995 deadline was missed, but implementation discussions are continuing.)

Alberta is considering the granting of similar authority to community health nurses. (*Canadian Family Physician*, August 1994, p. 1475.) In 1993/94, the Alberta government expressed support for a request by the Alberta Nurses Association for the use of nurses as first-contact professionals. British Columbia and Newfoundland are experimenting with the use of nurses in independent primary care roles. Saskatchewan has indicated a wish for greater care delivery by nurses. (*Medical Post*, March 12, 1996, p. 54.)

Fifteen publications on expanded roles for nurses have been summarized by Gerald Richardson and Alan Maynard. ("Fewer doctors? More Nurses? A Review of the Knowledge Base of Doctor-Nurse Substitution", Discussion Paper #135, Centre for Health Economics, The University of York, England, June 1995. The studies reviewed by Richardson and Maynard are listed at the end of this chapter.) Much of the literature is described as being weak in research terms, but it is unanimous in its findings. In general, studies report that between 30% and 70% of the tasks carried out by primary care physicians could be performed by nurses. There is a general consensus that substitution is not detrimental to health outcomes.

There were 20,000 nurse practitioners in the United States in 1986. (Kerr, J., and J. McPhail, *Canadian Nursing: Issues and Perspectives*, McGraw-Hill Ryerson, 1988.) Nurse practitioners have prescribing privileges in a number of American states (Ellis, J.R. and C.L. Hartley, *Nursing in Todays World*, J.B. Lippincott, 1992.)

Experience suggests that many primary care nurse practitioners will, in their practices, serve specific population groups such as children, women or the elderly, and/or deal primarily with selected types of problems (e.g., psycho-social, psychiatric, maternity care). The extent to which primary care nurse practitioners should be encouraged to specialize in one or more clinical fields is unclear, but specialization appears to be attractive.

Nurses have, in various ways, illustrated their ability to deliver primary care. In 1994, in Peterborough and in Ottawa, the Victorian Order of Nurses (VON) established incontinence clinics staffed by nurses supported by a urologist advisor. The clinics were established without provincial funding. Users paid over $500 for assessment, information, advice and a plan for improvement. (*Ottawa Citizen*, October 25, 1994)

The services offered by the nurse-staffed incontinence clinics are covered by provincial insurance plans only if provided by a physician. When the services provided in nurse-staffed clinics are provincially funded, then they will be well accepted, well used and perhaps less expensive than the same services provided by a physician. Whether such clinics will increase public expenditures on health care will depend largely on whether payments to physicians fall to offset the cost of the clinics staffed by nurses.

Nurse roles in secondary and tertiary care

Nursing specialization is well established, and the need for it is equally well established. Institutional care is increasingly complex and increasingly distinct from community nursing. Within community nursing, different skills are required for health promotion, care of the chronically mentally ill, care of the seriously physically ill (including palliative care) and social support. Within institutions, a different set of skills is required for intensive care nursing, obstetrical nursing, rehabilitation nursing, psychiatric nursing, etc.

No nurse can be competent in the full spectrum of clinical settings. The common base of knowledge and skills which nurses acquire in their initial training is an excellent foundation on which to build special knowledge and skills, but the specialist streams in nursing are now as distinct and separate as are the specialist streams in medicine.

The differences among nurses are recognized in the specialty organizations they form and the magnitude of the memberships of these organizations. The American Association of Critical Care Nurses had 57,000 members in 1988. Nurses in "independent practice" in Canada are not recognized as a specialty because they practice in a number of different fields, but they have common concerns which are best served by a common organization. There are estimated to be 1600 to 2000 nurses in independent practice in Quebec alone. (*Visions* – The newsletter of Nurses in Independent Practice in Canada, August 1994.)

Nurses who work in one clinical field tend to have skills quite different from the skills of nurses in other fields, and the differences will become even more pronounced as specialization becomes more formal and more prevalent. It is already unreasonable to expect a nurse with ten years of obstetrical, rehabilitation or operating room experience to join the staff of a pediatric ward and be competent as a pediatric nurse. Lateral mobility will be even less reasonable as more and more nurses become midwives, case managers, endoscopists, psychiatry practitioners, emergency care specialists, etc.

The career ladders which will best serve the public and best reduce present levels of dissatisfaction among nurses will be associated with higher levels of competence in a limited range of situations. The number of applicants to Canadian nursing schools has fallen, as has the grade point average of the applicants. Expansion of the opportunities for nurses to acquire higher levels of competence in their chosen clinical area(s) will increase the attractiveness of the field.

The importance of nurses with special skills was recognized as long ago as 1972, when a Canadian Nurses Association (CNA) Task

Force on specialization noted that policy makers and employers perceived a need for nurses with specialized skills. Almost 20 years later, about half of the advertisements for nurses ask for applicants with a particular skill. (J. Calkin in Baumgart and Larsen, *Canadian Nurses Face the Future*, Ch. 17, p. 327.)

The term "clinical nurse specialist" is, in most nursing literature, reserved for nurses with clinical training in masters programs. De facto clinical nurse specialists have, however, existed ever since general duty nurses acquired special skills by working in one clinical service in a hospital (such as pediatrics or obstetrics) or in the office of a physician specialist.

Nurses have also improved their clinical specialty skills through formal training other than at the masters level. Early examples include the neurosurgical nurses made famous by Dr. Wilder Penfield and the Montreal Neurological Institute, the psychiatric nurses of the western Canadian provinces, the nurse midwives, the graduates of the public health certificate programs, the pediatric nurse specialists which were pioneered in Colorado and the nurse anesthetists still in use in the United States.

Recent years have seen an increase in the number of university-trained clinical specialist nurses. In the fall of 1994, the University of Toronto began accepting nurses into specialization programs in Hematology/Oncology and Burns/Plastics (information from a personal communication from Marilyn Ballantyne CNS/NP, July 12, 1994). McMaster University has programs in at least nephrology and neonatology. A variety of specialist courses are now being offered in university and community college nursing schools in most provinces.

An Ontario Ministry of Health document in late 1994 recommended roles for nurse practitioners in secondary and tertiary care. The Ministry of Health recommendations mirrored those made in an earlier McMaster University report. (Mitchell, A., J. Pinella, C. Patterson and D. Southwell, *Utilization of Nurse Practitioners in Ontario*, September 1993.) The McMaster report recommended that nurse practitioners play a role in secondary and tertiary care in mental health, gerontology, long-term care, oncology, cardiac care and pediatrics. These areas were selected because of medical resident reductions, expanding demand, perceived physician shortages and Ministry of Health priorities. (To date, no action has been taken on this recommendation.)

Financial arguments favour early attention to expansion of nurse roles in secondary and tertiary care. The incomes of specialist physicians are significantly higher than those of family physicians. Payments to specialists in 1995 in Ontario represented 60% of all fee-for-service payments to physicians. (*Ontario Medical Review*, February 1996, p. 44.) Substitution of nurses for specialist physicians should bring greater reductions in cost than will accrue from substitution of nurses for primary care physicians.

Services to be transferred from specialist physicians to specialist nurses, whether in obstetrics, dermatology, urology, geriatrics, dialysis, diabetes or any of a number of other fields, will usually be easily identified. The value of the services to be transferred will usually be able to be costed reasonably quickly and reasonably well, and the ability to estimate the dollars associated with the services being transferred is important. Estimation of current spending on the services being transferred will allow transfer of funds from the global fund used to pay physicians to the global budgets of whichever agencies or providers become responsible for the services.

When a service has a specific cost (as with a cystoscopy) or a known average cost (as with care of a woman during pregnancy and delivery) the amount of funds which should be transferred out of the physician fund will usually be merely the number of services times the average cost of the service when provided by a physician, less the cost of physician back-up. This approach should be defensible for anesthesia, minor surgery, consultations, acting as a surgical assistant, interpreting X-rays, maternity care, immunization and diagnostic procedures such as PAP smears.

Secondary and tertiary care is often provided to referred patients. The patient may choose the person to whom they are referred, but often the choice is made by the professional who made the referral. It may be easier to encourage referrals to nurse specialists than to alter patterns of primary care delivery, although this is entirely conjecture.

The ability of adequately trained nurses and other professionals to safely and competently deliver complex health care is fully established, but questions of quality will still be raised.

The type of training and experience required to assure competence may be easier to determine when the role of the nurse specialist is clearly circumscribed. It may also be easier to obtain agreement regarding such things as which drugs and investigative procedures should be able to be ordered by a nurse specialist than to define the degree of authority which should be given to nurses in generalist primary care roles.

Studies have reported clinical and economic benefits from greater use of clinical nurse specialists. (Georgeopoulos, B. and L. Christman, "Effects of clinical nurse specialization: A controlled organizational experiment", 1990.) The use of nurse Case Managers in the care of patients with fractured hips at the Toronto Hospital resulted in cost reduction and outcome improvement. Some hospitals use nurses in the formal education of patients. (Budge, C., and S. Nelson, "A Deficit in Care – The Educational Needs of Thoracic Patients", *Professional Nurse*, October 1994, pp. 8-13.)

The factors described above may make it easier to introduce nurse specialists in large numbers than to introduce primary care nurses in large numbers.

The competence of primary care nurse practitioners is not being questioned in the preceding paragraph. As described earlier, nurses have proven that they can be fully competent in primary care roles. The arguments in favour of emphasizing transfer of specialist rather than primary care roles are tactical, financial and legal, but implementation of changes will at times relate more to tactics, money and legislatures than to whether a particular type of service can be adequately provided by nurses.

The literature on nurse specialization suffers from a significant weakness. The literature reports on studies of specialization rather than on the extent to which de facto specialization has occurred. Much of the powerful evidence supporting substitution of nurses for physicians comes from the way health care is now delivered, not from studies reported in the literature. Health care delivery is filled with transfers of function which have largely occurred because physicians wanted them to occur. The ease with which these transfers were made, and the adequacy of the service after transfer, suggest that many more functions could also be transferred.

Many of the trends now in progress are not new, and today's needs are not new. The following quotes are from an article in *The Canadian Nurse* 30 years ago.

> "For today's nursing we need formally trained specialist nurses. How many kinds, I really do not know. Perhaps we need psychiatric nurses, pediatric nurses, general surgical nurses, operating room nurses, intensive care unit nurses, obstetrical nurses, neurosurgical nurses, public health nurses, home care nurses, rehabilitation nurses and nurses prepared for nursing research, education and administration. On the other hand, perhaps some of those categories named do not merit separate postgraduate educational programs, (for example, public health nurses may now be adequately prepared for home care nursing; or a surgical nursing course might include

O.R., I.C.U. and general surgical nursing instruction). Perhaps there may be unmentioned categories that do merit separate teaching programs. In either case the principle of specialization remains.

The principle of specialization has already been recognized in those undergraduate and postgraduate courses specifically designed to educate psychiatric nurses, obstetrical nurses, public health nurses, neurosurgical nurses, nurse educators, nurse administrators and probably others, and for years hospitals have recognized the special value of the self-taught or specially trained nurse who has extra clinical competence. Despite these examples, however, the principle of the "specialist" clinical nurse is not widely represented in nursing education."

"In today's world of departmentalization and specialized technology, we need only a minority of nurses with major competence in more than one clinical field. Nurses with general rather than special competence are, and will continue to be, essential in smaller hospitals, and they probably will always be of value in the larger hospital in certain capacities, but it is desirable that we recognize that in larger hospitals and programs the patient will be served best by the specialist nurse working with the nursing assistant and other ancillary personnel as a nursing team."

"What are we currently asking of our graduate professional nurse? We ask that she be able to assess the nursing needs of a patient; that she be able to draw up a nursing plan to satisfy these needs; and that she be able to supervise and contribute to the application of this plan. These capacities are essential if nursing care is to be of high quality.

It is my assumption and belief that different knowledge and experience are necessary for these duties to be performed in different clinical circumstances, and that, therefore, some part of the nurse's education should prepare her for the particular problems of an identifiable clinical type of patient. Such preparation may lead to a happy situation in which nurses will be more content, employers more satisfied, and patients better cared for. Nurses will be more respected and more confident because they will be more competent. High school students contemplating nursing as a career may find nursing more attractive and nursing students or graduates who wish to stay at the bedside will be able to do so with proper competence, prestige and income. Recruitment may be increased and functional areas of special suitability to male nurses may be identified."

"If nurses during training or employment develop personal preferences for a certain clinical field or fields (and this seems likely); and if a significant number of nurses wish to work at the bedside (and I hope they do); and if nurses tend to be regularly assigned to one ward or service (and this is common); and if patients are to be congregated by clinical type (and this is inherent in our present hospital organization); and if most hospital beds are to be in institutions large enough to have at least one ward for each major service (and this is already the case); then we should as much as possible encourage nurses to have special competence in one clinical field. Scientific and technical advance has required the production of professional and technical specialists in many fields, but we still train general duty multi-functional nurses somewhat adequate in everything but with special competence in nothing."

"We have a number of options. We can educate nurses for general duty nursing or for nursing with a specific clinical orientation. We can teach them to be solo workers, team members or entirely supervisory in function. We can assign responsibility on the basis of what has been taught, or we can attempt to prepare for the responsibilities that will be given.

Surely we prefer to utilize nurses to do what most of them apparently want to do and certainly what they are most needed for... high quality, specialized, professional nursing. If so, do we wish to assure the

special clinical skills by formal postgraduate education or by on-the-job training? Surely the former."

(Sutherland, R.W., "Needed: Nurses who are Clinical
Specialists", *The Canadian Nurse*, September 1966.)

The options and preferences described in that 1966 article still
apply, although the environment in which decisions are being made
is very different from that of 1966. The challenge for nurses and for
other health care professionals is to establish those programs, and
promote those statutes, which will allow Canadian patients and
communities to fully benefit from modern health care provided at
the lowest possible cost.

How many nursing specialties should there be?

There will never be full agreement as to the most appropriate number of nursing specialties and subspecialties. Nurses are likely to
follow the physician practice of regularly recognizing new specialties; and a specialty, once recognized, seldom disappears. The number of recognized nursing specialties will, therefore, gradually
grow. (There are 45 to 60 recognized physician specialties, depending on which jurisdiction is being described.)

The Canadian Nurses Association has proposed that specialization
can occur when there is: (a) a body of special knowledge; (b) written
standards of practice and role description; (c) a prerequisite basic education and workplace; and (d) employer recognition of the specialty.

Nursing specialties could correspond to physician specialties, or
they could be different. There could, for example, be nurse endoscopists who perform a number of different endoscopic procedures
such as cystoscopies, sigmoidoscopies, bronchoscopies and gastroscopies. There is no equivalent specialty among physicians.
Another option is to distribute endoscopic procedures to nurse specialists in a manner which corresponds to physician specialization.
Nurse urologists would perform cystoscopies; nurse gastroenterol-
ogists would perform gastroscopies, etc.

The Canadian Nurses Association and the Royal College of
Physicians and Surgeons have specialty identification and evaluation processes. The approval of nursing specialties should respond
to the preferences and needs of employers, payers and consumers as
well as nurses.

The impact of changes in nurse roles

Many effects could flow from the changes discussed in this chapter
and elsewhere (Figure 4.2).

Figure 4.2

Probable Effects of New Roles for Nurses

On government spending on health care - No change

On user access to publicly funded services - Improvement

On family physicians - Lower total public spending on family physicians services; perhaps fewer billing numbers; perhaps lower average incomes

On specialist physicians - Lower total public spending on specialist services; fewer billing numbers; perhaps lower average incomes

On physician access to billing numbers - Fewer physicians with billing numbers

On educational institutions - Major changes

On how users see health care - Very little change

On user satisfaction - Very little change

On hospitals - Very little effect

On the law - New legislation and regulations will be needed

On Physiotherapists, Occupational Therapists, and other providers (other than physicians) - little effect

---

Possible expansions of nurse functions have been described, but the possibility of shrinkage of nurse roles should not be forgotten. A variety of technicians and therapists (both new and existing) could displace nurses in dialysis, rehabilitation, operating suites, psychiatric services, emergency departments and other locations and situations.

Summary

The roles of nurses have been expanding steadily for decades, and the expansion will continue. The central questions are how fast and how far the expansion should go, and how far and how fast it will go.

Primary care is usually the only field mentioned when expanded roles for nurses are being discussed, but there is even greater potential for expanded nurse roles in secondary and tertiary care.

Expanded roles for nurses will bring very few changes to the working lives of at least 90% of nurses. Most nurses will continue to care for patients in hospital. Others will continue to work in the community (in palliative care, home care, public health, health promotion and disease prevention) in much the same way as they do now.

Nursing has for several decades emphasized the importance of university degrees for all nurses and a master's degree as the vehicle for higher levels of competence. The degree of responsibility and skill inherent in nursing easily justifies the wish for a baccalaureate degree as a basic qualification for all nurses, but degrees do not automatically bring higher levels of respect, competence, income or usefulness.

Barriers to direct patient access to nurses have been discussed. These barriers were described by the Alberta Association of Registered Nurses as legislative, regulatory, policy, funding, values and beliefs and communications/integration. To these I would add semantic confusion, professional rigidity and professional timidity.

Any wish by nurses to avoid competition and confrontation between nurses and physicians, while also seeking access to more health care dollars and greater opportunities for independent health care delivery by nurses, is futile.

Efforts to define "nursing" are also a waste of time. It is much more important to expand the roles of nurses than to expand the boundaries of nursing. The delivery of health care, especially of publicly funded care, should be by whoever can deliver adequate services most cost-effectively.

Some of the concerns which exist among nurses and nursing students regarding changes in roles are unjustified. For nurses who are concerned that there will be a forced change in their careers, a numerical safeguard has been described. It is both necessary and unavoidable that most nurses will, in the future, continue to practice nursing in much the same way as it is currently being practised. For those who are concerned about the inability of nurses to be successful when they come in conflict with physicians, there is now a statutory model (the Ontario legislation) which creates a more level playing field. Power has been redistributed. For those who fear a loss of the "caring" focus which has been a characteristic of nursing, there is the reassurance that although some of the new roles for nurses will be technical, there will also be ample opportunity for expansion into new roles which are not technical. It also is quite possible for technical services to be provided in a caring manner.

Expanded roles for nurses in the delivery of health care will be welcomed by almost everyone. Almost everyone wants health care to bring greater value per dollar spent, and greater use of lower-cost providers is one way to improve cost-effectiveness. Changes which lower the cost of delivering health care can allow reallocation of funds to other services which also are important to health. Reallocation within health care could allow additional funding to services which currently have a high priority but low funding, e.g., health promotion.

Consumers, communities and payers will welcome increased opportunities for competition between providers and greater choice for consumers. Nurses will welcome increased career opportunities and a reduced likelihood of unemployment.

This chapter has not been constrained by whether a particular health care service has historically been, or is now, the domain of one professional or another. It has paid no attention to whether a particular service or activity is usually thought of as a nursing versus a medical versus a chiropractic or physiotherapy activity. These artificial distinctions are of no consequence to the user or the payer. The user simply wants a satisfactory service and the payer would merely like to be sure that the services purchased are reasonable value for money spent.

Chapter 4 has not assumed that nurses are inferior to physicians, or vice versa. It has not assumed that physicians are so powerful that nurses must defer to them, nor has it assumed that nurses are so perfect that the world will be saved by them. It has assumed that change is possible, that actions can affect the nature of the change, and that well-planned change will bring Canadians greater value per dollar spent on health care.

The health care studies reviewed by Richardson and Maynard, 1995.

Brown, S., and D.E. Grimes. *Nurse Practitioners and Certified Nurse-Midwives: A Metaanalysis of Studies of Nurses in Primary Care Roles.* American Nurses Publishing, Washington, 1993.

Bureau of Health Manpower. *Cost-effectiveness of Physician's Assistants in a Maximum Substitution Model.* US Department of Commerce, National Technical Information Service. Contract No. 231-760601. Prepared for Kaiser-Permanente Medical Care Program, 1976.

Denton, F.T., A. Gafni, B.G. Spencer and G.L. Stoddart, "Potential Savings from the Adoption of Nurse Practitioners in the Canadian Health Care System", *Socio-Econ Plan Sci*, Vol. 17, No. 4, pp. 199-209, 1983.

Ekwo, E., M. Daniels, D.O liver and C. Fethke, "The Physician Assistant in Rural Primary Care Practices", *Medical Care*, Vol. 17, No. 8, pp. 787-795, 1979.

Fottler, M.D., "Manpower Utilization Practices in Physician Offices", *Journal of Health and Human Resource Administration*, Vol . 5, No. 2, pp. 159-185, 1982.

Gavett, J.W., A.R. Jacobs and C.L. Thurber, "Physician Judgments and Resource Utilization in a Private Practice", *Medical Care*, Vol. 11, No. 4, pp. 310-319, 1973.

Knickman, J.R., M. Lipkin, S.A. Finkler, W.G. Thompson and J. Kiel, "The Potential for Using Non-physicians to Compensate for Reduced Availability of Residents", *Academic Medicine*, Vol. 67, No. 7, pp. 429-438, 1992.

Levine D.M., L.L. Morlock, A.I. Mushlin, S. Shapiro and F.E. Malitz, "The Role of New Health Practitioners in a Prepaid Group Practice", *Medical Care*, Vol. 14, No. 4, pp. 326-347, 1976.

Lomas, J. and G.L. Stoddart, "Estimates of the Potential Impact of Nurse Practitioners on Future Requirements for Physicians in Office-based General Practice", *Canadian Journal of Public Health*, Vol. 76, March/April, pp. 119-123, 1985.

Marsh, G.N. and M.L. Dawes, "Establishing a minor illness nurse in a busy general practice", *BMJ*, 310, pp. 778-80, 1995.

Rabin, D.L. and K.K. Spector, "Delegation potential of Primary Care Visits by Physician Assistants", Medex and Primex, *Medical Care*, Vol. 18, No. 11, November 1980.

Record, J.C., M. McCally, S.O. Schweitzer, R.M. Blomquist and B.D. Berger, "New Health Professionals After a Decade and a half; Delegation, Productivity and Costs of Primary Care", *Journal of Health, Politics and Law*, Vol. 5, No. 3, pp. 470-497, Fall 1980.

Salisbury, C.J. and M.J. Tettersell, "Comparison of the work of a nurse practitioner with that of a general practitioner", *Journal of the Royal College of General Practitioners*, 38, pp. 314-316, 1988.

Schneider, D.P. and W.J. Foley, "A Systems Analysis of the Impact of Physician Extenders on Medical Cost and Manpower Requirements", *Medical Care*, Vol. 15, No. 4, pp. 277-297, 1977.

Spitzer,W.O., D.L. Sackett, J.C. Sibley. R.S. Roberts, M. Gent, D.J. Kergin, et al, "The Burlington Randomized Trial of the Nurse Practitioner", *N Eng J Med*, 290, pp. 251-256, 1974.

CHAPTER 5

Expanded Use of Existing Health Care Professionals other than Physicians and Nurses

C hapter 4 examined expanded roles for nurses. Nurses were given a chapter of their own because changes in their utilization will affect the future of health care more than changes in the utilization of any other provider.

There are also, however, other health care professionals whose roles might change.

Athletic therapists and kinesthesiologists

These workers are officially unrecognized, although the skills of some of them have been considered adequate for employment by Olympic teams and athletic therapy centres. Some are highly trained, and their special skills are particularly relevant in this age of sports medicine. Standardization of educational programs and some form of professional designation would allow these providers to take their place in the health care team.

Audiologists and Speech Language Pathologists

In Ontario these professionals can assess and treat patients but cannot legally "communicate a diagnosis to a patient". This statutory anomaly should be corrected so that practice can be consistent with the law.

Chiropodists and podiatrists

The roles of chiropodists and podiatrists appear to be unlikely to change significantly, although relevant statutes may need amendment. In Ontario, podiatrists can legally "communicate a diagnosis to a patient" but chiropodists cannot, a difference which is difficult to explain.

Midwives

Most provinces have expressed general support for a greater role for independent midwives. In several provinces midwifery is legal.

All provinces should legalize midwifery and provide public funding for midwife services. Ontario has recently expanded midwife training opportunities and has insured their services under medicare (see Chapter 8, maternity care section, for further comment).

Optometrists

Optometrists wish authorization to treat a broad range of common eye conditions, and to have this treatment covered by provincial insurance plans. In 1996 New Brunswick passed legislation which authorizes optometrists to treat eyes with drugs. Saskatchewan has almost completed the same process and Alberta is considering similar legislation. Optometrists are able to treat eye conditions in almost all states in the United States.

In Ontario, Ministerial approval of changes in the regulations under the Optometry Act is all that is required to allow optometrists to provide eye care. The optometry legislation authorizes optometrist treatment of conditions listed in the regulations, but a list of conditions has not yet been prepared. Physicians have opposed allowing optometrists to use drugs in the treatment of diseases of the eye.

No province has approved payments to optometrists for services other than refractions.

Optometrists both test eyes and sell glasses. Physicians consider this to be unethical. Physicians are not permitted to have financial ties to a pharmacy or a diagnostic facility (e.g., a laboratory) to whom patients are referred, and an ophthalmologist is not permitted to sell glasses or be financially involved with an optician to whom patients are referred.

The optometrist conflict of interest is, however, roughly equivalent to that of a surgeon who assesses a patient, recommends surgery and then performs the surgery. It also is comparable to a situation in which an audiologist assesses hearing loss and then recommends use of a hearing aid which is sold by the audiologist or his/her employer. The conflict of interest which exists in these two situations (and others) does not raise questions of ethics.

Recent Ontario experience has raised concerns regarding the utilization of optometry services. For many years there has been no indication that Ontario residents lacked access to eye testing, and no indication that needed testing was not being done. In recent years, however, there has been a steady increase in billings by optometrists for refractions. Because the global fund for payments to optometrists has been frozen since 1992/93, the increase in the volume of billings has resulted in an expected 11 to 12% claw-back of payments to optometrists in 1996.

The recent increases in optometrist billings in Ontario may be more a product of increases in the number of registered optometrists than an increase in need. The optometrist supply has, in recent years, increased at 2 to 4% per year. In 1996, the increase was over 6%, i.e., from 941 in 1995 to 1001 in 1996 (Ontario College of Optometry, July 1996).

Concerns regarding over-servicing by fee-for-service optometrists could encourage governments to promote optometry services provided by salaried optometrists (e.g., in Community Health Centres). Concerns regarding over-servicing also could discourage approval of an expanded scope of practice for optometrists.

Optometrist fees for eye testing (refractions) are currently roughly the same as, or slightly lower than, the fees charged by ophthalmologists. Governments and other third-party payers would have an incentive to favour optometrists as the suppliers of insured eye testing if there was a significant fee difference between optometrists and ophthalmologists.

Paramedics

Paramedics are trained to offer a broad range of life sustaining and life protecting emergency services. Their skills are now being used in hospital emergency departments as well as in ambulances.

Roles of paramedics have, to date, evolved through physician delegation. Physicians have authorized paramedics to use intravenous drugs and fluids and operate defibrillators. The practice of having to consult a physician before providing services beyond first aid is now obsolete.

The supply of paramedics is quite limited. Training programs will need to be expanded if paramedics are to have significantly expanded roles in emergency care.

Paramedics cost more than less-trained ambulance staff. This extra cost has delayed their widespread use.

In Ontario paramedics are not among the professions with self-governing status.

It may be reasonable to increase the integration of the training and upgrading of ambulance staff and emergency room staff.

Pharmacists

As many as half of all prescriptions written for pharmaceuticals are inappropriate. This misuse of drugs increases cost and is a hazard to patients.

The causes of drug misuse include inaccurate and high-pressure marketing by drug companies, the pressures associated with fee-for-service practice, the number of drugs available, a physician culture which includes a tendency to use drugs whether or not they will be useful, the frequency with which information changes, the lack of good sources of information and the lack of use of the sources of good information which are available.

It is asking too much to expect prescribers to know all of the uses, interactions and side effects of the hundreds of drugs in regular use. It is reasonable to expect prescribers to routinely seek advice, and the major sources of advice will be pharmacists and computer software.

In most teaching hospitals and some long-term care institutions, pharmacists are part of the team which determines how drugs will be used. They review charts, review physician drug use profiles and visit the wards. Pharmacists attend clinical meetings (rounds) as experts in the pharmaceutical field. Pharmacists and physicians, working together, have improved prescribing. Drug use guidelines and protocols (some of which are mandatory) protect patients and lower costs.

The pharmacist/prescriber partnership will eventually include prescribers other than physicians, and it will expand into community health care. Expanded roles for pharmacists will become even more desirable as more health care professionals acquire the right to order prescription drugs.

Provincial, regional and institutional drug utilization management programs have been shown to improve the quality of prescribing. These programs use both education and regulation to reduce drug misuse and lower costs. They will become more common in the near future and pharmacists will play key roles in them.

Pharmacists should become a major source of advice to all who prescribe pharmaceuticals, and to the persons who are having their prescriptions filled. This will require less involvement of pharmacists in the filling of prescriptions. This change, which is already well on its way, is supported by pharmacists and their associations. Even more of the dispensing function will eventually be delegated to pharmacy assistants. Advice to professionals and clients, and the protection of users and payers, will become the primary pharmacist functions. Expenditures on pharmacy assistants will increase, but the increases in cost will be more than offset by reduced expenditures on drugs.

Unlike expansion of the roles of some other health care providers, expansion of pharmacist roles has produced very little conflict. The expansion does not reduce the scope of practice of other professionals and it only minimally reduces the autonomy of professionals with prescribing powers.

Changes in legislation will usually not be needed to permit expanded roles for pharmacists.

Users will not notice the increased involvement of pharmacists in prescribing decisions. Users will welcome a greater role for pharmacists as advisors.

There will be little if any need for changes in pharmacist training programs. Universities are already preparing pharmacists for an expanded role.

Physician Assistants (PA)

Physician Assistants in the United States work primarily in physician's offices and usually under the supervision of a physician. There are 59 accredited PA programs in the United States, and six job offers for each graduate. (*Observer, American College of Physicians*, December 5 1994, p. 6.) Physician Assistants are not trained in Canada, nor does any province recognize them in any official way.

The formally trained PA is an option to the less-trained (or untrained) persons who often staff physician's offices. Both the formally trained Physician Assistants and those who are less trained may perform many office procedures, including such things as PAP smears and prescription renewals. (Fisher, I., "Doctors assistants and what they do in the Netherlands", *World Health Forum*, Vol. 15, 1994, pp. 269-270.)

There appears to be little likelihood that formally trained Physician Assistants will become part of the Canadian health care team, but they could.

Physiotherapists

The diagnostic and therapeutic skills of physiotherapists are proof of the competency which can be the product of a specialist baccalaureate program.

Physiotherapists can, in several provinces, see patients without referral from a physician, but they cannot prescribe drugs or order laboratory or other investigations. Only in British Columbia, Alberta and Ontario can private physiotherapists bill the provincial insurance plan, and even in these provinces there are sharp limits on the number of private physiotherapists who are allowed to bill.

Physician referrals to physiotherapists seldom ask for a particular type of service. The physiotherapist is usually expected to assess the patient, establish a diagnosis, define a treatment plan and carry it out.

Physiotherapy has some of the characteristics of physicians services. There tends to be a concentration on physical health, an emphasis on procedures, a tendency to always treat and a tendency to treat extensively whether or not the cost-effectiveness of the treatment has been proven. Physiotherapists on fee-for-service, or who work for an agency paid on fee-for-service, deliver more services per day and more services per patient than are delivered by physiotherapists whose services are not paid for by fee-for-service.

Much of what many physiotherapists do is repetitive and not complex (e.g., massage, passive and active range of motion, established exercise routines). These functions could be delegated to less-skilled personnel such as physiotherapy assistants (who may be called Certified Therapy Assistants) and aides.

Physiotherapists wish the right to bill medicare and prescribe drugs.

It is unclear whether they will, or should, function as first-contact professionals rather than as professionals to whom patients are referred.

Psychologists, medical/psychiatric social workers and other trained counsellors

Changes in the roles of these health care professionals will seldom come from new skills. Their skills are already adequate. They already provide services equivalent to most of the therapeutic, preventive and diagnostic mental health services offered by physicians. Changes will, if they come, come from greater recognition of existing skills and from elimination of discriminatory health insurance payment policies.

Most mental health services can be provided by more than one type of health care professional. This invites the use of health care delivery teams and it invites competition. At the moment, very few of the advantages of competition can be realized because legislation and payment policies place physicians in a very favoured position.

Competition between physicians, social workers, psychologists, psychiatric nurses and some counsellors will become more complete when two policy changes are put in place. First, nonphysician

providers (after additional training if necessary) need to be authorized to provide some services which are currently reserved for
physicians (such as the use of prescription drugs). Second, and of
greatest importance, all competent professionals must have equal
access to public funding of their services.

If all mental health professionals had equal access to public funding, where would governments find the money?

Governments could increase total spending on health care.
Payments to physicians for services such as counselling and psychotherapy could then be maintained at present levels while also
making payments to psychologists, social workers and others. This
option is unlikely and undesirable. Total spending on health care
should not increase.

Governments could transfer money from other health care sectors
(such as drugs, optometry, ambulances, physicians or hospitals) to
the services of psychologists and social workers. This is possible.
Some of the needed funds might be found this way.

Reductions in payments to physicians could occur in three ways.

Governments could require users to pay part of the cost of mental health services regardless of which provider was involved.
Public payments to physicians would go down, and payments to
psychologists and social workers would be less than if there were
no user fees. This also is a possibility.

Governments could take steps to reduce the delivery of psychotherapy and a variety of counselling services by family physicians with little or no special training in these fields. This would
release funds for payments to more qualified personnel.

Governments could also limit their payments for psychotherapy
and counselling to the cost of the lowest-cost provider. This would
probably mean that public payments for many mental health services
would be at the cost of services provided by social workers. This is
a good option, especially if combined with other policies to prevent
increases in total costs. Users would have more choices and professionals would be treated more equitably. Providers who wished to
charge more than the cost of the lowest cost provider could be
allowed to extra-bill, or there could be no payment to providers who
would not accept the public payment as payment in full.

Radiology technologists

With only modest additional training, X-ray technologists could
competently read most X-rays of extremities, face, chest, spine,
pelvis and abdomen, and many ultrasound images. Technologists in
the armed forces are taught basic interpretive skills, and similar

skills could be developed in civilian technologists. Technologists would refer films to a radiologist when interpretation was in doubt, and such a referral could be mandatory in specified circumstances. Certain kinds of X-rays would continue to be routinely interpreted only by radiologists and other appropriate physicians.

The interpretation of X-rays and ultrasound images by radiology technicians (or other health care professionals other than physicians) will require either changes in legislation or physician authorization.

Education for the technicians (or others) who will interpret the X-ray or ultrasound images will be a problem only if radiologists refuse to provide it. Radiologists could also refuse to provide back-up for technicians.

Lower costs should be easy to accomplish. An experienced technician would diagnose and describe a fractured finger, forearm or nose in about the same time as would be required by a radiologist, and the costs per hour of the two professionals are very different.

Experience will establish whether technicians who read films should continue to also provide traditional services such as the taking of X-rays. A mixed role appears to be feasible but not mandatory.

Summary

Expanding the roles of health care professionals other than nurses and family physicians will usually affect only one sector of health care.

Expanded roles for pharmacists are likely to be widely accepted in the near future.

The roles, in mental health services, of social workers, psychologists, psychiatric nurses and other trained counsellors should be expanded. In addition, government payment policies should be amended to remove discrimination against these professionals.

Expanded roles for radiology technicians could offer almost immediate savings and would be easy to implement.

Human resource policy options should be evaluated in terms of their ability to: (a) give all competent providers a relatively equal opportunity to provide insured services; (b) allow consumers to receive care from the qualified provider of their choice; and (c) reduce total public expenditures on health care.

CHAPTER 6

The Education Options

As the roles of health care professionals change, initial training and continuing education will also change. There may be changes in where training occurs, the length of initial training, how training is funded, the approach to learning, the nature of the curriculum, the degree of integration of programs, the number of graduates and how competence is maintained over time.

This chapter discusses the initial preparation and the upgrading and renewal of health care professionals. As in other chapters, considerable attention is given to nurses.

Initial versus continuing education

Educational programs for health care professionals prepare individuals for employment and/or assist them to maintain competence over time. Individual programs decide how much to emphasize initial versus continuing education.

The rapidity with which knowledge and skills become obsolete, and the frequency with which individuals change their roles, suggest that education throughout one's professional life is more important than initial training. What is learned during one's initial training should be supplemented or replaced regularly with skills and knowledge pertinent to new eras and new roles.

Both initial training and continuing education might give consideration to the following description of how competence is gained and lost.

> "From unconscious incompetence (we don't know that we don't know)
> To conscious incompetence (we know we don't know)
> To conscious competence (we take steps to be sure we do what is best)

To unconscious competence (we automatically do what is right)"

(Hayes, B.J., *The New Paradigm: Concepts and Application in Public Health Nursing*, June 1994, pp. 150-154.)

The above sequence will, over time, automatically lead to step #5, the reappearance of unconscious incompetence (and the cycle begins again). It would seem preferable to remain constantly in phases two and three, and emphasis on continuing education is most likely to keep health care providers in these phases.

Studies in Australia and Sweden have shown that the year of graduation is the most dominant determinant of how physiotherapists treat stroke patients. (Carr, J.H., S.F. Musgrove and others, "Physiotherapy in Stroke Rehabilitation: Bases for Australian Physiotherapists Choice of Treatment", *Physiotherapy Theory and Practice*, December 1994, pp. 201-209.) In other words, the physiotherapy which is provided to patients is predominantly the physiotherapy which students learned about in their undergraduate program. The initial training of physicians has also been shown to be a major determinant of the decisions made by physicians.

The dominance of initial training should end. Health care will be more appropriate if there is at least as much attention to continued learning as to initial learning, and if spending on continued learning is as generous as spending on initial learning.

The adequacy of a professional five, ten, twenty and forty years after graduation depends primarily on his or her working environment and on the efforts made to remain up-to-date. Continuing competence is more a product of hands on experience, opportunities to continue to learn and a personal willingness to continue to learn, than of the initial curriculum. The skill with which any professional can deliver a baby, read an X-ray, counsel a dysfunctional family or assist a community to change its lifestyle is neither assured by a particular introductory curriculum or ruled out because of deficiencies in that curriculum.

The functions of an introductory education are to provide a reasonable initial degree of user safety (through the presence of an acceptable initial degree of provider skill and judgment), to help new graduates understand and identify with their chosen work and to prepare graduates for life-long learning.

With experience, introductory skills and judgment become more mature. Maturation of skills and judgment occurs at the bedside, in the community and in the office rather than in the classroom.

Top-down versus student-centred learning

Initial education is not as important as some educators think it is, but it does influence the delivery of health care. The manner in which initial education is offered is therefore of consequence.

Too many university and community college programs still use the classical education model of classrooms, memorization and teacher control. This model persists despite the knowledge that the greatest current need is for problem solvers who can adapt to change and to the appearance of new challenges. Educational programs must choose between education which emphasizes the absorption of information and education which emphasizes the ability to solve problems.

The top-down memorization approach to education is not appropriate when learning must be a life-long activity. It does not prepare students for either the independent or the collaborative decision making processes which are central to the delivery of modern health care.

Fortunately, there is now a well-established educational option. The Cleveland Western Reserve and McMaster model of practical problem solving and independent study is, after decades of open or subversive rejection by the establishment, finally becoming the preferred approach in medical schools. (Burrows, G.N., 50th annual meeting of the Association of Canadian Medical Schools, *ACMC Forum*, December-March 1994, pp. 1-4.) Nursing, physiotherapy and other programs are also converting to an emphasis on problem solving and independent study.

The McMaster model of learning is patient-centred from day one. It allows considerable flexibility in what the student emphasizes and the way it is learned. It invites students to become analysts. It assumes that the problems and the environments which will be faced in one's professional life will constantly be changing, and that independent problem-solving skills are, and will be, more useful than yesterday's information.

Specialization

Specialization can be a product of education, experience or a combination of the two. It may begin immediately upon entry into post-secondary education or it may be added to a generic base of professional education. It may be the product of on-the-job experience, formal education or a combination of these.

Nurses, dentists and physicians receive a generic training. This generic training may then be followed by specialization. To a lesser extent the same sequence applies to a number of other health care professionals.

It is an accident of history that dentists, nurses and physicians train first as generalists. They could have followed a different path. If specialization during initial training had been chosen, medical and nursing students would be trained to deal with only one type of problem or patient. Pediatric nurses would be trained in a program separate from the program producing surgical nurses, and psychiatrists would train in a program separate from the program which produces surgeons. Psychiatrists would presumably not learn much bacteriology, obstetrics and surgery, and surgeons would learn very little about psychiatry. All physicians and nurses would be specialists.

It is also an accident of history that physiotherapists, chiropodists, respiratory therapists and others acquire skills in only one clinical field. These special skills could just as easily have been obtained in programs which built on some form of generic introductory education.

Specialist clinical skills can be the product of:
- a community college program (as with most dental hygienists, ambulance staff, laboratory technologists, chiropodists and psychiatric nurses in the western provinces);
- a baccalaureate program (as with physiotherapists, optometrists and some midwives);
- a graduate non-degree program (as with nurse practitioners in Alberta, Nova Scotia and the new Ontario programs);
- a graduate degree program (as with clinical psychologists, medical social workers, most speech language pathologists, some clinical specialist nurses and some nurse practitioners);
- a doctoral program (as with many clinical psychologists) or,
- on-the-job experience, i.e., an apprenticeship program (as with specialist physicians).

Physician specialists are the highest earners and are the health care providers who are seen as the most qualified, but their specialty programs are only marginally within the formal educational system. The training is in a workplace, and the specialist qualifications are granted by the profession rather than by an educational institution. Specialist physician training recognizes the value of experience in a real life setting. There are few classroom elements in the programs leading to physician specialization, a feature which has not reduced the value or acceptance of the specialist qualification. The success of the physician model should not be ignored when opportunities for specialization are being designed for other professionals.

Specialization during initial training

Many community college and undergraduate university programs produce health care specialists, e.g., respiratory therapists, laboratory technologists, physiotherapists, dental hygienists, nonnurse midwives, optometrists, chiropodists, occupational therapists and psychiatric nurses.

In the psychiatric nursing programs in the western provinces, the first year is shared with students in the Registered Nurse stream. In Saskatchewan, these programs enrol 110 to 120 students per year. Graduates can obtain an RN with one year of additional study. Great Britain, France and Belgium offer similar psychiatric nursing programs which are separate from the RN programs. (Roemer, M.I., *National Health Systems of the World*, Vol. 2, 1991, p. 25.)

Other undergraduate nursing programs may, through electives, allow some degree of specialization. In some programs in the United Kingdom, for example, a student nurse may, after 18 months of "Common Foundation", enter a specialty stream such as pediatrics. They may also continue with specialist training after graduation as an RN. (Hunter, J., "Revamping British Nurse Education with Project 2000: Focus on Children's Nursing", *Pediatric Nursing*, September/October 1994, pp. 439-442.)

Undergraduate nurse specialization has its down side. As students are given opportunities for academic concentration on clinical areas of interest, there is less attention to other clinical areas. A nurse might graduate with little or no exposure to obstetrics, surgery or occupational health. The range of general competencies (the "core" competencies of nursing) shrink as opportunities for specialization increase. (This is not assumed to be bad, it is just a fact.)

Specialization which builds on a generic education

Specialist skills may be obtained in diploma or certificate programs, or in master's or post-master's programs, which build on an initial general education. In nursing, three to four per cent of recent nurse graduates (250 to 300 per year) proceed to a master's degree (although only 1% to 2% of the total nurse population have a master's degree).

Nurses with master's degrees have definitely added to the teaching and research capabilities of the nursing profession, but they have had only a very limited effect on the delivery of health care because their numbers are small. They have, however, served one important purpose. They have demonstrated the adequacy with which nurses with extra training can provide advanced and independent patient care.

The tendency to see master's programs as the desirable place to prepare for advanced nursing roles has probably impeded the evolution of nurses into those roles. Master's programs tend to emphasize theoretical work and/or produce only a few graduates per year. The impact of a small number of graduates on the delivery of health care cannot be great even if all of them become service providers. The effects are even less when many graduates accept positions in teaching, research and administration.

Joy Calkin, PhD, (in Baumgart and Larson, *Canadian Nurses Face the Future*, p. 325) states: "it is likely that a Masters Degree in a specialty area will be required for certification in the future." If Dr. Calkin is correct, then the probability that specialist nurses will play major new roles in the delivery of health care is decreased. If specialist nurses are to become a dominant work group, as they should, then there must be an opportunity for at least 1,000 to 2,000 nurses to become clinical specialists each year. Recent decisions in Ontario support specialization without obtaining a graduate degree, and nurses' associations appear to be tacitly if not openly supporting this approach.

Master's programs which prepare clinical specialist nurses should opt for the "professional" master's model. In this model, which is currently used by MBA and MHA programs, there is an emphasis on work-related courses. (The teachers are, unfortunately, often persons who may have little or no practical experience in the fields about which they teach, but the educational model is sound.) These programs give little attention to general educational courses, emphasize practical rather than academic content and usually do not require theses. They see their graduates as practitioners rather than researchers and educators.

The "professional master's" model may include a period of on-the-job experience, a component which would seem to be essential for clinical specialists.

Current master's programs in nursing graduate only about 200 nurses per year. This number might, if the programs are significantly altered, be able to be increased to the 1,000 or 2,000 that are required, but it appears to be easier and more manageable to offer specialization programs which do not lead to a master's degree.

Clinical specialist training after receiving a master's degree in nursing is not common, but it was offered at the University of Toronto in 1994-95 in response to a request from nurses and their employers. A three-month course upgraded the skills of about 40 nurses already working in pediatrics, burns and plastics, orthopedics, geriatrics, trauma, cardiology, oncology, adolescent care, pain management, nephrology or palliative care. Many of these nurses were trained to perform functions previously performed by medical residents. (Simpson, B., "The Acute Care Nurse Practitioner Program: A Collaborative Effort", *Registered Nurse*, December/January, 1994/95.) It is likely that this kind of upgrading of nurses already working as specialists will become more common, but it does not seem necessary to limit enrolment to nurses who have master's degrees.

Primary care nurse practitioners are now being trained in each of the ten Ontario university nursing programs. The ten programs enrolled a total of 140 students (75 full-time equivalents) in the first year (1995). It appears likely that graduates of the new nurse practitioner programs will be able to practice autonomously in primary care and will be authorized to communicate a limited range of diagnoses to patients, order a limited range of diagnostic tests, prescribe a limited range of prescription drugs and refer to all types of specialists. These programs do not lead to a master's degree. They are open to nurses with a baccalaureate or a diploma RN. A diploma nurse requires two years of training to become a nurse practitioner; a baccalaureate nurse requires only one year.

In 1996, Ontario also created a special one-shot opportunity to allow nurses already in independent practice to upgrade their skills and qualify for the new nurse practitioner functions. Evaluation for entry into the special program placed greater value on practical experience than on academic qualifications. Applicants to the upgrading programs (many of whom were nurse practitioners) were evaluated primarily on the basis of the roles they had recently played in the delivery of care, rather than on whether or not they had an advanced academic qualification.

In 1995, 35 nurses at the Saskatchewan Institute of Science and Technology graduated from a one-year program in advanced community nursing. This program for nurses is designed to prepare nurses for work in the North, but with 34 graduates a year the North will not be able to absorb them all. These nurses are designed to work under the supervision of physician preceptors, but the Saskatchewan Medical Association (SMA) does not support the program. The SMA called these nurses the beginning of a two-tier health care system, presumably meaning that the nurses will provide inferior care. If physicians do not cooperate, the required preceptors may not be available. Unless the nurses become legally able to practice without the supervision of physician preceptors, they may join the dental therapists as professionals who have needed skills but who have difficulty finding employment.

Nursing is not the only profession which produces specialists by building on a generic education. A generic program in social work may be followed by a clinical Masters in Social Work, and a baccalaureate degree in psychology may be followed by a master's degree or a PhD in clinical psychology.

Informal specialization

Experience plus continuing education programs is the route most commonly followed by nurses who acquire specialist skills. In the absence of large scale opportunities for specialist preparation in formal courses, nurses and others obtain the necessary skills in whatever way possible.

Clinical skills can be improved by taking university and community college credit and noncredit courses. Topics include gerontology, mental health, geriatrics, palliative care, intravenous therapy, community nursing, emergency care, footcare, critical care and public health.

Hospital-based nurse specialization programs are not new. The Montreal Neurological Nurse training program was an early example. In 1974, the University of Alberta Hospitals established the position of Nephrology Nurse Clinician and prepared nurses for this specialized role. These nephrology nurses continue to be used and their functions have expanded. Their tasks include patient histories and physical examinations, arterial punctures, insertion of peritoneal catheters, endotracheal intubation, writing orders for medication, ordering X-ray and laboratory examinations, and referring patients to other hospital services. (Molzahn, A.E. and J.B. Dosseter, "The Nephrology Nurse Clinician: A Unique and Expanded Role for Nurses", *Dialysis and Transplantation*, November 1988.)

The Spring 1994 issue of *Kaleidoscope*, a publication of The Hospital For Sick Children in Toronto, states:

> "Another initiative laid out in the strategic plan calls for Sick Kids to develop alternate care models: this means teaching nurses or other professionals to perform certain types of care that have usually been carried out by doctors."

The nature of the educational programs proposed by The Hospital For Sick Children is not identified, but the programs are likely to be hospital designed and delivered and consist of a mix of academic sessions and practical experience. The training of paramedics also combines mandatory field training with academic training, but this program is based in a community college rather than a hospital.

Some specialist training programs require clinical experience in the relevant area before acceptance into the specialization program. The Canadian Nurses Association, for example, requires one to four years of relevant recent work experience for recognition of nurses as specialists. The amount of required experience can be less for individuals with post-basic academic specialty training.

When considering the process by which specialist professionals are produced, and when considering the training options, it can be useful to look outside of health care. Outside educational examples can suggest that health care programs over-educate some students.

Air traffic controllers have one of the most responsible and stressful occupations. No other professionals routinely and repetitively make decisions which are crucial to the lives of so many people. These practitioners are specialists in the field of aviation, but they don't know how to fly a plane or land a plane. They are trained only to do the job that they do, and they often are not trained in a college or university. This example does not infer that a college or university education is a waste of time or that education should not be obtained in colleges and universities. It does suggest that specialists can make important decisions and perform complex tasks without having studied the full range of tasks which are related to their own and without having been trained in an institution for higher learning.

The approval of specialties

The Canadian Nurses Association has approved seven nursing specialties, i.e., emergency, nephrology, neuroscience, occupational health, critical care, perioperative and psychiatric/mental health. The CNA sets standards for the specialty groups and determines which nurses will be permitted to call themselves specialists.

The Royal College of Physicians and Surgeons, and their counterpart in Quebec, control the identification of physician specialties. Both conduct examinations for those seeking specialist designations. There are now over 50 approved specialties. The College of Family Physicians of Canada performs the same functions for physicians who wish to be certified as family physicians.

The funding of education

Changes in the way health care professionals are utilized will mean changes in educational costs. Some new costs will be incurred establishing new training programs (such as those for Ontario midwives). Other new expenditures will be needed to expand and/or upgrade the skills of existing workers.

Most post-secondary education in Canada is provided by private, nonprofit institutions with a high degree of public funding, i.e., universities, colleges, hospitals, public health units, family practice units and community health centres.

Physicians in recognized internships (a term which may be disappearing) and specialty training programs were paid between $30,000 and $53,000 per year (1995-96) (Association of Canadian Medical Colleges, 1996). The practice of paying professionals while in apprenticeship programs could be applied to other professionals.

Privately financed programs play a small role in the education of health care professionals. Many chiropractors are graduates of private, for-profit programs, as are graduates of the Canadian School of Management (which offers a Masters in Health Administration) and some private technical schools.

Funding formulas may need to be amended so that they encourage greater attention to continuing education and greater recognition by programs of prior education and learning.

The educators

Clinical education is usually provided by senior colleagues in the same field, i.e., physicians train physicians and nurses train nurses. This model has deficiencies when a profession is moving towards competence in fields which formerly were the exclusive domain of someone else. Who should train nurses, for example, to become nurse anesthetists? It will be difficult to rapidly graduate large numbers of clinical nurse specialists and advanced level nurse practitioners unless some of the required skills are taught by physicians and pharmacists. (In some programs, these outside professionals are already fully involved.) Similarly, radiologists will be required to train X-ray technicians to read X-rays.

Nurses can be the educators of other professionals. In Britain, "epilepsy liaison nurses" visit the offices of general practitioners to give advice regarding epilepsy protocols, the use of registries and the opportunities for interaction with hospitals and other sources of care. (*Professional Nurse*, February 1994, p. 296.) Nurses could play similar roles with respect to skin care, ostomy care, palliative care and care of the chronically ill.

The development of curriculum

Curriculum development is characterized by conflict.

One conflict is between a general education and a career-related education. If programs which graduate health care professionals place major emphasis on "the well rounded and educated individual", then there will be attention to history, languages, philosophy and/or other fields which have little direct relationship to the professional competencies which are central to the delivery of health care. It is highly probable that a broad education does promote maturity, tolerance, leadership and thoughtfulness, but there is an inevitable tension between the wish for a curriculum which emphasizes job-related skills and a wish for the intellectual growth associated with a more generic education.

There can also be conflict between basic sciences and more work-specific material (the applied sciences). In medical schools there has been a decrease in the number of hours allocated to some basic sciences such as anatomy and biochemistry.

In many programs there is also constant jockeying between different specialty elements. It is difficult to know how many medical school hours should be assigned to ophthalmology versus orthopedics, etc. It is equally difficult to know how many hours in the optometry program should be assigned to physics versus marketing, and how many nursing program hours should be assigned to pediatrics versus adult care.

Curriculum development is usually controlled by academics, but practitioners, students, employers and the consumers of health care have a legitimate interest in it. Involvement of all affected players is probably best. All evaluations of programs, graduates and continuing education have a degree of validity.

Academics should not be allowed to dominate curriculum development. They tend to give excessive attention to theory, may wish to cover more material than students can assimilate and may teach much which is not relevant to the careers of the students. Academics may, however, be more aware of (and certainly should be more aware of) the current literature, the recent developments in the field and the developments which are likely to occur in the future. They also should have the broadest view of the field and be less prone to emphasize only one part of a field.

Everyone should seek a reasonable relationship between educational programs and public goals. When thought necessary, politicians and bureaucrats can and should use legislation, regulations and funding to move educational programs in a desired direction. Politicians and bureaucrats should be participants in curriculum review and revision, even if only to maintain close contact between educators and those who regulate and fund the programs.

Students, alumni and the community can also contribute. Students and alumni have important things to say about whether the quantity of material is tolerable, whether the format in which it is presented is consistent with the objectives of the program and whether regurgitation of information is seen as more important than thought.

Curriculum decisions are made difficult by the historical emphasis on facts rather than decision making, by our poor understanding of the relationship between education and performance, by an underemphasis on continued learning, by uncertainty regarding the roles which graduates will play and by teachers who lack the practical experience required to make the education relevant.

Control of the supply of health care professionals

Provincial ministries which are responsible for the regulation and funding of universities and colleges have the ability to determine how many students will be enrolled in publicly funded programs. This regulatory and financial power, when combined with the almost complete absence of privately funded universities and colleges in Canada, provides provinces with a much greater ability to control health care manpower supply than is possible in the United States (where most universities and colleges are privately funded).

When physician supply was considered to be inadequate in the 1960s provincial and federal governments cooperatively created a number of new medical schools. In the 1990s, the same national cooperation led to an agreement to reduce medical school entry by 10%, a reduction which took place almost immediately.

The high level of public control over our educational institutions means that provinces can, on short notice, either enlarge or shrink the numbers of entrants into medicine, nursing, optometry, etc. This ability led to the establishment in 1995 of nurse practitioner programs in all ten Ontario university-based nursing schools and to the establishment of three midwifery programs. Provincial governments could, in the same way, decide to expand graduation of clinical specialist nurses or establish programs to prepare radiology technicians for the interpretation of X-rays.

Ability to control enrollment numbers does not mean that demand for specific professionals will equal supply. Critics complain about public money being spent educating health care professionals who cannot find a job after graduation, but unfortunately human resource needs usually cannot be accurately predicted. It is routine to graduate (at public expense) school teachers, cooks and historians who cannot find a job, and the same lack of fit between supply and demand will always apply to health care providers.

In general, it would appear preferable to have a modest oversupply of most professionals than to have an undersupply. It is always a tragedy when anyone who wishes to work is unemployed, but the tragedy is no greater or smaller when the unemployed person is a nurse, physician or physiotherapist rather than a computer analyst, an architect, a teacher or a librarian.

Isolation versus integration of educational programs

It is believed that training can affect the skill and willingness with which professionals work together. (This is a hunch more than a proven fact.)

Health Science Centres were promoted 30 years ago as a device to integrate the education of various health care professionals. This integration was supposed to lead to greater teamwork and greater understanding by each profession of the roles of other professionals. In the end, however, not much changed when health science centres appeared. Some administrative integration occurred when Deans of Health Sciences became responsible for several programs, but the administrative merging seldom led to integration of significant components of the academic curriculums or of the related field experiences.

The isolated approach to education is epitomized by speech therapists (speech language pathologists), respiratory therapists, audiologists, chiropodists, podiatrists, physiotherapists, nurses, occupational therapists, midwives (when they are not also nurses), dentists, chiropractors, optometrists, allopathic physicians, osteopathic physicians and most of the other health care workers. There is very little joint teaching, few expressed regrets that programs are so isolated, minimal transferability of credits from one program to another, minimal sharing of faculty and very little joint research.

There is a remarkable similarity between much of the material taught to physicians and that which is taught to nurses, physiotherapists and some other health care professionals. The discussion of pharmacotherapy in nursing text books, for example, is remarkably similar to the level of understanding expected of medical students (see such books as: McFarland, G.K., and M.D. Thomas, *Psychiatric Mental Health Nursing*. Ch 39, 1991; Hickey, J.V., *Neurological and Neurosurgical Nursing*, 3rd Edition. Lippincott, 1992; Haber, J., A.L. McMahon, P. Price-Hoskins and B.F. Sideleau, *Comprehensive Psychiatric Nursing*, 4th Edition. Mosby,

1992.). Despite the similarity of the material taught, the programs which graduate health care professionals are miles apart. Isolation is preferred, and there is little indication that it will decrease.

The isolation of the programs which graduate health care professionals need not apply to programs aimed at upgrading skills. Continuing education programs can be, and sometimes are, offered to a mix of providers. The Portsmouth Health Care Trust in England offers an introductory course in diabetes which is aimed at junior physicians, nurses, podiatrists, dietitians and others. (*Professional Nurse*, October 1994, p. 7.). Primary care update programs are often attended by a mix of physicians and nurse practitioners, and the mix will increase as more professionals offer independent care. Conferences and workshops in mental health, rehabilitation, public health, counselling and health promotion are routinely attended by a mix of professionals.

Urban needs versus the needs of isolated communities

Developing new roles for nurses and others has at times been seen as a way to bring health care to isolated communities which cannot support or attract full-time physicians. This objective led to the outpost nurse practitioner programs at Dalhousie University and the University of Alberta.

Special preparation for nurses who will work alone is desirable. Without nurses with competence in a broad range of primary care, isolated communities might have no local health care at all. The programs which graduate professionals who will work in isolated communities do not usually, however, graduate personnel appropriate for new roles in the urban settings in which most Canadians receive their care.

The focus of this book is on the preparation of professionals for new roles within urban hospitals and communities. In these settings sophisticated back-up is expected rather than impossible. Changes in urban health care must bring good health care at a lower cost, whereas the objective of the outpost programs is the delivery by professionals of at least some primary care in locations in which there would otherwise be none.

Summary

Education for personal caregivers can be user-centred or disease/organ-centred. It can teach respect for the rights of the user or it can promote the preeminence of the caregiver. It can aim for a competent problem solver, a well-rounded and educated graduate prepared for leadership, a competent technocrat, a team player, someone who has established her or his ability to absorb and regurgitate information, someone who will work alone, someone who will work only under the supervision of others or some combination of these. It can be dominated by the importance of degrees or by the importance of the functions to be performed.

The environments in which professionals work affect the extent to which practising professionals remain up to date and acquire new skills. Decisions made by those who organize, supervise and evaluate care, and who assist established professionals to remain competent, may therefore be more important to ongoing competence and optimal public service than are the introductory educational programs.

A relevant introductory academic curriculum, an emphasis on independent responsibility and problem solving, and a workplace environment with appropriate resources and opportunities for ongoing learning appear to be more important for public safety than the duration or location of initial preparation or the qualifications granted at the end of it.

The line between concepts and skills is not clear, and both have value, but the field requires care providers with advanced clinical skills and an understanding of when and how these skills should be used. Educational planners should keep these requirements in mind when deciding where and how health care workers are to be trained.

It is a mistake to concentrate on initial training and neglect continuing education and on-the-job training. Any professional who concentrates on one field will develop expertise in it, assuming that there is reasonable attention to keeping up to date and an inherent wish to learn and to be competent. The level of expertise will, however, be higher and more sustained if employers, funders and professionals appreciate the need for structured, accessible and relevant continuing education.

The Pew Health Professions Commission, in its 1991 Report titled *Healthy America: Practitioners for 2005; An Agenda for Action for United States Professional Schools*, states that the Report was "inspired by the belief that the education and training of health professionals is out of step with the evolving health needs of the American people." This quote also applies to Canada, and Chapter 6 has explored some of the ways through which Canadian educational programs might respond to discrepancies which exist between education programs and health care needs.

CHAPTER 7

Funding and Payment Options and Their Effects on Provider Roles

How health care providers are paid, and how their employers are funded, are among the factors which alter the roles of health care providers.

Individual providers can be paid by salary, sessional fee, fee-for-service, capitation or some combination of these. Agencies and institutions can be funded by a global budget, a line-by-line budget, fee-for-service, capitation or some combination of these. The implications of these funding and payment options are examined in this chapter, as are some financial policies and practices of Ministries of Health.

Funding flexibility within a Ministry of Health

Ministry of Health budgets are divided among the many sectors of health care, e.g., mental health, hospitals, emergency care, community services and health promotion. Each sector has its own budget or fiscal envelope. When it is difficult to move funds from one envelope to another, policy options are restricted.

Ministries can move money relatively easily between envelopes when the Ministry can unilaterally adjust prices and/or shrink or expand the global budget of a health care sector. Provinces can move money easily from hospitals to community services, for example, because the allocations to hospitals are set annually by the Ministry, there are no agreements or statutes limiting the movement and hospitals are accustomed to having their allocations reduced. A ministry can, if it wishes, merely decide how much money it wishes to add to the budget for community services and then remove that sum from the institutional envelope.

On other occasions, ministries cannot easily transfer funds from one sector (or sectoral envelope) to another. Ministries move money with difficulty when a particular envelope is governed by some sort of agreement. Many provinces, for example, have signed agreements with their provincial medical associations. These agreements may establish the amount which will be spent annually by the province on physicians services. The agreements may also describe the way in which the annual payments will change. Some province/medical association agreements have been as long as seven years, e.g., Ontario and British Columbia.

Provinces can, with legislation, override their agreements. (The Ontario seven-year agreement was abruptly terminated by the government in 1996.) The agreements do, however, when honoured, reduce the ease with which a province can introduce new approaches to health care delivery.

In Ontario, the former seven-year agreement with the Ontario Medical Association stated that the global physician payment envelope did not include payments made to physicians on salary in Community Health Centres (CHC). This clause in the agreement contributed to the slow growth of CHCs in Ontario in the period 1990 to 1995. Ontario wished to significantly increase the number and size of CHCs, but doing so would have increased the total expenditures on physician's services. The global allocation for fee-for-service physicians would not have gone down as total salaries paid to CHC physicians went up.

If a Ministry of Health cannot move money easily from one envelope to another, the addition of a new health care provider can increase financial pressures. Payments to midwives in Ontario, for example, are an add-on cost. Many of the services provided by midwives were formerly provided by physicians, but the global fund for physicians is not reduced to compensate for payments to midwives.

Transfer of function without an associated transfer of funds leads to either a reduction in expenditure somewhere else in health care or to an increase in provincial expenditures on health care. Most provinces have now decided that the budgets of Ministries of Health should not grow. If funds from the physician global budget are not used to pay for services being provided by midwives the funds for midwife services must come out of hospital budgets, ambulance budgets or the expenditures made for some other Ministry-funded service.

Physicians are zealously protecting every dollar within the global cap on fee-for-service payments. They vigorously oppose use of the global fee-for service fund to pay for services which have been transferred to physicians who are not on fee-for-service, or which have been transferred to professionals who are not physicians. The Ontario Medical Association even opposes using the physician fund to make payments to physicians with respect to referrals from midwives and nurse practitioners (*The Medical Times*, The Ontario Medical Association, July 1995).

The Ontario Medical Association decision regarding payments for referrals from nurses and midwives is strange. There has never been any objection to allowing the physician global fund to be used for services provided to patients referred by dentists. Whether this strange decision is the product of global capping of payments to physicians is uncertain. It is quite possible that it reflects nothing other than a punitive and self serving mindset which intends to pretend that the delivery of health care is not in the midst of fundamental change. Fortunately, this recommendation was not implemented.

The limitations imposed by agreements such as those between provinces and medical associations make it desirable that the provinces and the professionals who wish an expanded role plan carefully to be certain that changes are ready to be introduced at the time that an agreement expires.

The moment of expiry of an existing contract would seem to be the best time for major reallocation of funds; it is a window of opportunity. Preparation for the reallocation of funds should begin long before expiry of the contract.

When a contract has expired, the province is in a strong position. It can, if it wishes, arbitrarily reallocate from one envelope to another without breaking an agreement it has signed.

The effects of global budgets

Global budgets can change the way health care providers deliver their services. Global budgets give agencies greater control over how their budgets are spent. Hospitals, public health units and others on global budgets have an incentive to use the lowest-cost provider who can deliver satisfactory service.

Hospitals, for example, are responsible for the costs of radiology services to in-patients. Payments to radiologists for interpretation of in-patient X-rays come out of the hospital global budget. If hospitals were legally able to have some of their X-rays read by radiology technologists instead of by radiologists, the cost of these services would go down. The hospital would have more of its global budget left to spend on other services.

In 1994, the medical teaching staff of Queen's University, Kingston, Ontario, and the medical staff of The Hospital For Sick Children, Toronto, traded fee-for-service payments from the

Ontario Health Insurance Plan (OHIP) for a fixed annual payment from the province. This change from fee-for-service to a global budget created a situation in which it is in the interests of the physicians and the universities to transfer functions to nurses and other nonphysician providers whenever possible. Physician income does not go down when activities are transferred to other professionals. The transfer leaves the physicians with more time for teaching, research or family. The university benefits from the increased availability of the physicians as teachers and researchers. The public is probably unaffected.

Sometimes the transfer of services to a lower-cost provider is not attractive to agencies such as hospitals and home care programs. If, for example, nurse responsibilities in dialysis units increase and physician responsibilities decrease, there may be additional costs to the hospital. There may be reduced billings from physicians to the medicare plan for dialysis services, but the savings (if they occur) will benefit the province rather than the hospital.

Even the provincial savings may be an illusion. The global budget for physician services is unlikely to go down just because physician billings for dialysis services go down; there will be offsetting increases in physician billings for other services.

The effects of capitation

The effects of capitation vary with who receives the capitation payments.

When providers (such as a physician group practice) receive a fixed sum per month or year for the care of a patient or a population, there is an incentive to minimize the volume and cost of services provided. Reducing the amount or cost of services delivered can be accomplished by such things as greater use of the telephone to follow up patients, greater use of lower cost providers, the promotion of lifestyles and skills which reduce the need for health care, the education of the consumer, early referral to other providers and/or conscious avoidance of user need and demand.

Fee-for-service encourages physicians to provide care themselves. Capitation encourages use of less expensive providers. If physician payment is by capitation, physicians benefit from greater delegation of tasks to other professionals.

The Ontario Medical Association Primary Care Reform Advisory Group recommended capitation as the method of payment for primary care, and in July 1996, the Minister of Health announced that this recommendation would be implemented in selected communities in 1997. Ontario has for a number of years funded a number of

Health Service Organizations by capitation, but in the new arrangement the capitation payments will apply to all primary care providers in a region.

To a provider paid on capitation, there is a penalty for providing additional care and for using expensive providers. The costs of operating the practice rise and/or the working day lengthens, but there is no increase in income. Whether there will be an increased use of nonphysician providers in the capitation communities remains to be seen.

When the capitation payment is made to an agency or organization, the agency is the direct beneficiary as costs are contained and it is the agency which is at greatest risk if costs exceed capitation income. Capitation provides an agency with an incentive to use the most cost-effective provider. It encourages the transfer of functions from physicians to other professionals.

In some Health Maintenance Organizations in the United States, the capitation income is collected by the agency but the staff physicians share in the risk and in the benefits. If costs are well controlled and agency income exceeds expenditures, the physicians receive a bonus at the end of the year. Physicians become allies of the agency in seeking to lower the cost of care. Both physicians and agencies are winners when care is delivered more cost-effectively. This encourages physician support for transfer of functions to lower cost providers. Fewer physicians will be employed, but those who remain may have higher incomes. Capitation may also lead to individual providers being penalized if their total costs per patient (including drug, hospital and referral costs) significantly exceed the costs generated by other providers caring for similar patients.

Regional health care budgets are similar to capitation in the sense that they are based at least partly on the size of the population being served. In this situation, the region has an incentive to use, or encourage the use of, the most cost-effective providers.

The effects of fee-for-service and payment ceilings

Physicians, chiropractors, optometrists and dentists may be the professionals who first come to mind when fee-for-service is discussed, but other health care providers also bill this way. Nurses in independent practice (and there are now thousands of nurses in Canada in this category) often bill on fee-for-service to patients or private insurance plans. (They are not eligible for payments from provincial medicare plans.) Private physiotherapy clinics bill on fee-for-service, as do some chiropodists and almost all alternative therapists (such as massage therapists, herbalists, acupuncturists and reflexologists).

Providers on fee-for-service are paid for each service they give. When payment is by a province, the fees are routinely set by the province. Gross income is determined by the number of services billed for (subject to "capping" when it is in place). If fees are reduced, providers tend to attempt to maintain their incomes by either increasing the number of services billed for per hour or by working more hours.

When rapid patient turnover is desired, persons who are slow to dress and undress, slow to answer questions and complex to treat can be financially unattractive to providers paid on fee-for-service. These patients may move through the office slowly, but their visits may not produce any more income than the visits of persons who move through quickly. The chronically mentally ill, persons with AIDS, the homeless, the confused, some physically handicapped persons, some addicts and the very old may not be welcomed as patients. This applies even when payment for the services is guaranteed by a universal insurance plan. (For some providers some of the above categories of patients are also culturally unattractive.)

The amount and type of health care which is provided changes when health care providers who are paid on fee-for-service can bill for services which are provided by employees. When a nurse in a physician's office administers vaccines or gives allergy shots the physician bills for each service. The physician increases income without personally being involved in more care.

In the period during which Ontario paid for hair removal (which is now not an insured service) there were dermatologists who hired a number of electrolysis technicians and billed for work done by these technicians. (With a cap on total payments to each physician on fee-for-service, this type of entrepreneurial health care is no longer possible.)

An annual or quarterly ceiling on the payments that a physician or other provider can receive from medicare also alters the delivery of care. If anything, there is an even greater incentive to be selective about the diseases and persons cared for. Patients who were unattractive when there was no ceiling on medicare fee-for-service payments become even less attractive when income is capped.

Services and patients not covered by medicare become more attractive when income ceilings exist. Income from sources other than medicare is income above the provincial ceilings. In addition, the fees received from sources other than the province are often higher than the fees paid by the province.

Will fee-for-service become more common?

Some nurses would like to practice independently and bill fee-for service to medicare, but two things must happen before this can occur.

First, it must be legal for the nurse to provide services as an independent practitioner. This is already the case so long as the nurse provides only "nursing" services.

Second, the provincial medicare plan must agree to pay for the services of the nurse on a fee-for-service basis. This could be done, but it is highly unlikely that any province will do it. Provinces do not wish to expand the number of practitioners paid by fee-for-service. In Ontario, the Ministry of Health has made it clear that the nurses currently being upgraded to work independently with advanced clinical skills will not be able to bill fee-for-service to the provincial medicare plan.

Fee-for-service is administratively complex and invites creative billing. A good understanding of the fee schedule plus judicious manipulations in the way services are provided can increase income without increasing office costs or consumer benefit and without lengthening the work day of the care provider.

The effects of payment by salary

Most health care providers are on salary, as are most workers outside of health care. Salaried professionals may be employed by other professionals, by an agency, by a government or by anyone else.

The productivity of salaried versus fee-for-service providers has often been compared. Findings vary, and interpretation of the findings is controversial. In Sweden and in the United Kingdom surgeons on salary provided lower volumes of service per day or month than physicians on fee-for-service, and the volume of surgery per salaried surgeon fell over time. Physiotherapists on salary see fewer patients per hour, and appear to provide fewer services per hour, than physiotherapists who either work on fee-for-service or are employed by employers who bill on fee-for-service. Physicians on salary in Community Health Centres see fewer patients per day than physicians on fee-for-service.

Providers on salary spend more time per visit with their patients. They probably see patients fewer times per year. Despite a lower volume of services, professionals on salary may be contributing at least as much, if not more, to the health status of their consumers (per dollar spent) as do the fee-for-service providers.

Summary

The way health care professionals are paid affects how much care is provided, the way care is provided and who gets the care. Fee-for-service appears to be the method of payment which most dramatically alters patterns of practice, but all other methods of payment also have effects. Funding and payment policies are, therefore, among the factors to be considered when examining new roles for health care providers.

In the short term, substitution of one health care provider for another seldom alters total Ministry of Health expenditures. The cost of one particular service, or one type of service, may change, but the changes are unlikely to affect the global budget of the Ministry. Similarly, the global budget (envelope) of a hospital or public health program does not change merely because the cost of something goes down or up. The significant change is in the amount of care which can be delivered with the money available. Lowering costs through the use of less expensive personnel (or through any other mechanism) will allow the same volume of services to be delivered with less money.

As policy makers contemplate role changes, they should wonder whether payment methods should also change. Should some payment methods be avoided? Which policy options increase (or decrease) the extent to which some health care providers can benefit from the employment of other providers? How do funding and payment choices affect the ability of governments to alter the utilization of health care professionals?

CHAPTER 8

Opportunities for Role Expansions

This chapter describes some of the opportunities for expanded roles for many types of health care professionals. It consolidates, adds to and/or supplements ideas found throughout many other chapters.

Some of the role expansions which are discussed have been tested by someone, usually a hospital, a clinic, a public health unit, a province, or an individual provider (usually a physician). The testing has not always been thorough, but some evidence is better than no evidence.

Other role expansions which are discussed appear to be sensible but appear not to have been evaluated. These possible expansions of roles deserve examination even although they are speculative. Common sense, plus awareness of experiences in similar, but not identical, situations, can identify opportunities for substitution.

This chapter does not discuss the transfer of functions from one physician specialist to another. These transfers are common as technology changes and as specialists compete for patients and services, but the transfers seldom have a significant effect on the cost-effectiveness of the delivery of health care. (For example, the role of radiologists in the investigation of coronary artery disease decreased when cardiologists assumed a larger role in invasive procedures such as angiography. [Link, K.M. and N.M. Lesko, "Cardiac Imaging", Guest Editorial, *Radiologic Clinics of North America*, May 1994.] If new noninvasive diagnostic tools such as magnetic resonancing replace invasive diagnostic procedures, the role of radiologists may again increase.)

Opportunities for altered roles are reviewed under a number of clinical headings. These headings are discussed in alphabetical order.

Abortion

Not all Canadian women have access to abortion services close to home. Many hospital boards have never permitted abortions and many regions do not have free-standing abortion clinics. In Cape Breton, for example, there was in 1994 not only no hospital which would allow an abortion to be performed; there were few physicians willing to refer a woman for an abortion (*Pro-Choice News*, January 1995). Prince Edward Island residents face similar deficiencies in their access to abortion services.

Access to abortion services has fallen in some communities due to an increase in physical attacks upon physicians and others associated with the performance of abortions.

Abortions could be safely provided by appropriately trained surgical or obstetrical nurses, or by surgical therapists. An increase in the number of health care providers legally able to perform abortions, especially if combined with an increase in the number of sites at which abortions are performed, would increase the likelihood that women who choose to abort an unwanted pregnancy would be able to obtain this medical service close to home. Use of lower-cost providers would also reduce the cost per case.

Addiction

In Canadian addiction units, both intake assessment and continuing management of cases are commonly carried out by social workers and nurses. Similarly, in some addiction units in England nurses triage new arrivals and they may, after triage, fully manage the case through to discharge (personal communication; Leeds Addiction Unit, 19 Springfield Mount, Leeds, England, April 1995).

Authority to order prescription drugs and investigative procedures would allow nurses and social workers to provide more complete management of persons with addictions.

Anesthesia

Nurse anesthetists became well established in North America during the 1930s. The United States Association of Nurse Anesthetists was founded in 1931. Nurse anesthetists provided the anesthesia for the world-famous blue baby operations in Boston in the late 1930s, and they are still recognized in many states in the United States.

Nurse anesthetists are not recognized in Canada, but they should be. Their use would be particularly appropriate in locations where physician anesthetists are available for back-up.

Physician anesthetist/anesthesiologist associations regularly ask Canadian provinces to increase the number of training spots for their specialty. The real or impending shortage of physician anesthetists might be eliminated by more careful selection of those patients for whom surgery is appropriate, but another solution would be to establish Canadian training programs for nurse anesthetists. It also would be possible to train anesthetists who are neither physicians nor nurses.

The Ontario Nursing Act provides unlimited authority to nurses to administer "a substance by injection or inhalation". It appears that no amendment is needed for nurses to administer anesthetic agents by injection or inhalation.

Case Managers

Nurse case managers have shown their competence in orthopedics, home care, chronic mental illness, congestive heart failure and many other specialty areas. Nurses can perform well as case managers in any field in which they have been trained and have experience.

Case managers require special skills and knowledge regarding the user group with which they deal. It is not reasonable to expect any one nurse or other professional to be an adequate case manager in a number of diverse clinical fields. Case managers in oncology, pediatrics, long term care, dialysis, community mental health, palliative care, etc., each require knowledge and experience specific to their field.

Community care

Nurses and other professionals who deliver community care become very knowledgeable of the environment in which care is being delivered. They become acquainted with the abilities, preferences and priorities of the patient and other household members as well as with the physical, social and economic environment of the home and community.

Community care providers – especially nurses, but also physiotherapists, occupational therapists, respiratory therapists and other providers – often serve patients for weeks at a time without contact with a physician. Their knowledge of the patient and of the home environment, plus the skills and judgment acquired through training and experience, makes them appropriate persons to be responsible for a broader range of community health care. With broader authority to order investigations and prescribe drugs and other therapies, with advice from consulting pharmacists, and with access to physician advisors when needed, these community-based professionals could deliver this broader range of services. The involvement of physicians in community care could become even less than it is now.

Dentistry

The children's dental care program in Saskatchewan in the 1970s and 1980s proved two things. First, providers with limited training and who are paid on salary can provide a higher quality of care than those with more training and much higher fee-for-service incomes. Second, dominant professions do not hesitate to use their power to serve their own ends. The political power of dentists led the Saskatchewan government to transfer the dental care of Saskatchewan children back (from less-trained but superior providers – the dental therapists) to dentists.

Expanded roles for both new and proven dental personnel (other than dentists) are indicated. In Saskatchewan the competition of the dental therapists lowered the cost of pediatric dental care provided by dentists. Competition throughout adult dental care could give consumers a choice and would probably lower costs.

Dermatology

The income of dermatologists is derived to a significant extent from a high volume of elective cases in which a few diagnoses, procedures and treatments dominate. Clinical situations of this type are ideal for the use of less expensive specialized personnel who do not have the broad introductory education of a physician or the extensive specialist training of a dermatologist.

A nurse could, with 6 to 12 months of specialty education and experience, adequately deal with many (and perhaps most) of the patients currently seen by specialist dermatologists. A separately trained therapist who is neither a physician or a nurse would need a longer period of training for the same level of competence. Dermatology therapists or nurses could diagnose and treat common skin conditions, perform technical procedures such as punch biopsies and provide advice to nurse practitioners and family physicians.

In Saskatchewan in 1992/93, 64,000 cysts, moles, scars, warts, granulomata, keratoses, papillomas and minor tumours were removed and billed to the medicare program at a cost of about $25 per case. Many of these minor procedures would, when performed by a dermatologist or other physician, be associated with an office visit or consultation fee. It cannot be assumed that a nurse or surgical technician would perform these procedures at a lower cost, but the volume and simplicity of the procedures makes it reasonable to examine the potential for use of less-extensively trained personnel.

Many of the dermatology services provided by dermatologists could be adequately provided by family physicians with a modest amount of training in community dermatology, but cost reductions associated with the use of family physicians would probably be less than the reductions associated with the use of specialist nurses or technicians.

Emergency care

Experience in many settings has established the competence with which nurses and paramedics can handle many emergencies.

Care at the site of an emergency is usually provided by nurses or ambulance staff. Care during transport in ambulances is provided almost exclusively by ambulance personnel. In hospital emergency departments, nurses and paramedics routinely perform triage (i.e., assess patients on arrival and determine their degree of urgency) and participate in continuing care. In many ambulatory care settings (such as Health Maintenance Organizations, Community Health Centres and the Armed Forces) nurses and paramedics provide complete care for many emergency patients.

The 1994 Report *Emergency Health Services Nova Scotia* recommended paramedics as the key personnel in the provincial and regional emergency systems. The report also recommended an "Ask-A-Nurse" phone line as a first-contact option. It was predicted that this phone line would reduce the number of requests for an ambulance.

An Ontario study recommended greater use of Quick Response Teams to reduce admissions to hospital through the emergency department. These teams would deliver services to the home in lieu of hospital care. Nurses, with their historical dominance as deliverers of community care, are logical leaders of these teams (Institute of Clinical Evaluative Sciences, Toronto, Working Paper #10, 1993).

The syllabus for the program for the training of emergency staff in Nova Scotia illustrates the high level of skill predicted for someone with two years of training. A graduate of Levels One and Two of the two-year course (the first 16 to 24 weeks) is expected to be able to manage childbirth and physical and mental emergencies including evaluation of a patient, evaluation of air entry, maintenance of an airway, performance of CPR (cardio-pulmonary resuscitation), immobilization as required, administration of oxygen, performance of automatic external defibrillation and attendance to catheters, intravenous lines and other aspects of patient care.

After another 12 to 18 months of training, a Level Three graduate is expected to more competently perform all level one and two activities plus initiate intravenous therapy including pressure infusion, use antishock garments, perform endotracheal intubation, monitor and interpret cardiac irregularities, use a pulse oximeter, perform manual defibrillation, administer intravenous medication and perform chest decompression (Conjoint Committee standards as provided in the Nova Scotia Emergency Health Services Report, 1994).

Level Three training produces a paramedic. Many provinces are expanding the presence of paramedics in ambulances. As the supply of paramedics increases, there will be extension of the present trend towards more clinical independence for ambulance staff.

A number of nursing schools are now offering credit courses in emergency care, and the number of recognized nurses specialized in this area is growing rapidly.

If the roles, responsibilities and legal authority of nurses and paramedics are expanded, many emergency room patients will be fully cared for without the involvement of a physician. This will reduce payments to fee-for-service emergency physicians. It will also alleviate the reported shortage of physicians trained in the delivery of emergency care.

Expanded roles for nurses and paramedics will require few, if any, additions to present levels of formal training.

Statutory and/or regulatory changes may be needed to authorize the ordering of investigations, the prescribing of drugs and the discharging of patients by nurses and paramedics.

Endoscopy

Endoscopic procedures include sigmoidoscopy, laryngoscopy, gastroscopy, bronchoscopy and cystoscopy. All of these are high-volume procedures. Most are performed by specialist physicians. All could be performed by a nurse or a technician with a modest amount of training.

In January 1994, the *New England Journal of Medicine* published a report describing the experience of surgeons who taught their nurse to perform sigmoidoscopies. The training was minimal and was informal, but the results were satisfactory. During a discussion in St. Johns, Newfoundland, in 1994 with Dr. Harry Edstrom, chest surgeon and incoming President of the Newfoundland and Labrador Medical Association, Dr. Edstrom spoke of a colleague in his specialty who had trained his nurse to perform bronchoscopies.

Physicians could delegate these endoscopic functions to nurses or others, but widespread delegation is not likely. These are bread-and-butter income generators in many physician practices. In Ontario, the Regulated Health Professions Act and the Nursing Act already provide authority for nurses to perform these procedures, but in most provinces legislative or regulatory changes would be necessary if these functions are to be transferred.

Geriatrics

Arguments in favour of greater team leadership from nurses and others have special applicability to the field of geriatrics. Geriatric assessments are routinely performed by public health nurses, and continuing care is then often provided primarily by nurses. The frail elderly usually present with a mix of medical and psychosocial problems which are not best handled by physicians. Nurses and social workers are already the main support for elderly individuals and their families, and an expanded scope of practice would increase their ability to provide high quality and low cost care.

Gynecology

A clinical nurse specialist or nurse practitioner gynecologist will, when legal impediments are removed, be able to provide competent and comprehensive care for many patients currently seen by family physicians and by specialist gynecologists. Vaginitis, dyspareunia, dysmenorrhea, infertility, birth control and many other problems which lead to visits to physicians offices could be effectively handled by less expensive, less interventionist and less pharmaceutically oriented personnel.

Midwives in Ontario are currently seeking the opportunity to provide primary gynecological care as well as midwifery services.

Hemodialysis (see nephrology)

Intensive care (see also neonatal intensive care)

In 1993, 774 nurses took the critical care exam sponsored by the Canadian Nurses Association (Visions, August 1994). Nurses are becoming increasingly involved in adult, child and neonatal intensive care, and this increasing involvement should be legally recognized.

Maternity care

It is estimated that less than 1% of Canadian maternity cases are handled by midwives. This compares poorly to the 75% of British deliveries which are handled by the 20,000 midwives working in the British National Health Service. (Roemer, M.I., *National Health Systems of the World*, Vol. 2, 1991, p. 26.)

There is powerful statistical evidence supporting an expanded role for midwives in Canadian obstetrical care. Commissions that have studied midwives tend to believe that midwives are more cost-effective than physicians, and that the quality of obstetrical care is improved by the introduction of midwives. (*Report of the Provincial Advisory Committee on Midwifery*, Province of Newfoundland, May 1994.)

> "...in countries with the lowest infant and maternal mortality rates, the great majority of childbirths are attended by trained midwives." (Roemer, M.I., op cit.)

American nurse midwives have been extensively compared to American physicians. Nurse midwives use less anesthesia and analgesia, induce fewer patients, do less electronic fetal monitoring, perform fewer episiotomies, use forceps less often, use fewer hospital days per patient and use fewer intravenous fluids. Caesarian section rates are the same, as are maternal and infant mortality rates. Nurse midwives provide more prenatal and postnatal visits. (American Nurses Association, "A Meta-analysis of Process of Care, Clinical Outcomes, and Cost-effectiveness of Nurses in Primary Care Roles: Nurse Practitioner and Nurse Midwives", December 1992.)

An article in *Ontario Medicine*, November 23, 1987 began: "A professor of obstetrics from the Netherlands said if he were a pregnant woman in Canada expecting to have a normal delivery he'd leave the country." Dr. Jelte DeHann said he would not stay and face the risks of surgical intervention. The caesarian section rate in The Netherlands was 5.5% at that time compared to about 20% in Canada. The use of surgical inductions, forceps delivery, episiotomies and major anesthesia was also higher in Canada. Maternity care in the Netherlands is provided primarily by midwives.

The amount of academic and practical obstetrical training received by midwives prior to entry to practice is greater than that of most family physicians. The entire working experience of the midwife is in the field of obstetrics, whereas family physicians spend only a minority of their time in that field. Continuing education of midwives is entirely in their chosen field, whereas family physicians must distribute their continued learning through pediatrics, mental health, emergency care, geriatrics, etc. After graduation, the obstetrical skills of the midwives must inevitably be better maintained than the obstetrical skills of most family physicians who practice obstetrics.

Financial comparisons of midwife services and physician services have been made, but not in Canada. In 1976/77, Blue Cross/Blue Shield of Greater New York reported total costs of maternity care provided by midwives in free-standing birthing centres as about two-thirds of the cost of care provided by physicians. Other similar data were as recent as 1986. (R.W. Lubic in "National Commission on Nursing Implementation Project: Models for the Future of Nursing", National League of Nursing, New York, 1988; Part 5; WY 5 N2775) These data are too old and foreign to be taken as proof that midwifery care will, in Canada, be less expensive than physician care, but it probably will be.

Midwife incomes will be lower than those of obstetricians, but the number of midwives needed to provide obstetrical services may be greater than the number of obstetricians who would provide the same services. Changes in hospital costs are not known, but they should go down. Even if costs per case are the same, the use of midwives will mean more people are employed, which is socially desirable. Greater consumer satisfaction is also an additional incentive for greater use of midwives.

The involvement of family physicians in obstetrics has been declining steadily in Canada, as has the percentage of specialist obstetricians who are practising obstetrics. Given the withdrawal of physicians from obstetrics, a withdrawal underway before midwives appeared on the scene, one would think that the transfer of obstetrical care to midwives could be accomplished without conflict.

The speed with which midwives replace physicians will depend partly on the supply of midwives. (In 1993, 62 midwives graduated from an Ontario upgrading program. These 62 became the total complement of midwives authorized to practice independently and with public funding in Ontario.)

The rapidity with which the supply of midwives can be expanded will depend partly on whether provinces prefer nurse midwives or midwives who are not also nurses. If the nurse-midwife model is chosen, large numbers of nurse midwives could be quickly available because the training resources exist, the training period would be one year or thereabouts, and there is a large pool of nurses from which the new professionals would be drawn. Direct entry midwives (the midwives who are not nurses), on the other hand, require several years of training. If midwives are to quickly provide much of the obstetrical care currently being provided by physicians, provinces should opt for the nurse-midwife option.

If the supply of midwives becomes adequate, and if legal and financial impediments to the use of midwives are removed, midwives could quickly provide the majority of Canadian maternity care. Unfortunately, only Ontario has expanded its midwifery training programs and provided public payment for midwife services.

Canadian physicians have, when faced with the legalization of midwifery, been guilty of many inane and discouraging comments, but these inappropriate reactions say a great deal more about physicians than they do about the adequacy of the care which trained midwives provide.

Mental Health

Psychiatrists, family physicians, medical social workers, psychiatric nurses and clinical psychologists all deal with a broad range of mental health problems. Counselling is routinely provided by the same personnel plus nurse practitioners and the clergy. The duration and quality of the training of these professionals in the handling of mental health problems varies considerably.

Many family physicians have had little or no formal training in psychotherapy or counselling. (*Ontario Medical Review*, September 1994, pp. 28-41.)

> "While some physician-therapists have sought training and supervision in psychotherapy, we have learned that many do not, and that the level of training and skill varies widely between individuals. It seems that many physicians believe that little or no special training is required to do psychotherapy." (*Final Report of the Task Force on Sexual Abuse of the College of Physicians and Surgeons of Ontario*, 1991, p. 116.)

Despite these concerns about the quality of their preparation, family physicians have become increasingly involved in the delivery of psychotherapy and other mental health services. A General Practice Psychotherapy Association, founded in 1984, had 1400 members in 1993. Problems dealt with include depression, anxiety, panic disorders, dysfunctional families, marital problems, obsessivecompulsive disorders and physical, sexual and emotional abuse. Family physicians in Saskatchewan in 1992/93 billed for almost 98,000 psychotherapy sessions. A typical patient received 20 to 25 sessions of psychotherapy.

Several hundred thousand Canadians have dementia. Much of the clinical decision making associated with care of these patients could be transferred from physicians to nurses with modest additional formal training (Proceedings of the Workshop on "The Challenge of Dementia in Canada – from Research to Practice", May 1993, *Chronic Diseases in Canada*, Spring 1994).

The 1991 cost of providing health care to patients with dementia has been estimated at over three billion dollars. (*Can Med Assoc J.*; 151(10): 1994, pp. 1457-64.) The magnitude of the total costs, the large number of patients involved and the often similar social and medical needs of the patients suggests that this is an area in which the role of nurses, social workers and other providers should increase and the role of physicians decrease. Outcomes will not change and costs will go down.

It is difficult to justify paying physician fees, especially specialist physician fees, for psychotherapy, counselling and other services which can be provided by other professionals at less cost. From 1972 to 1988, fee-for-service psychiatrist psychotherapy per 1000 population increased by 120% (*National Health Insurance and Private Psychiatry*, Health Reports, Health Canada, Vol. 3, No. 3, 1991). In a search for more cost-effective health care, mental health services should be given a high priority.

Transfer of services to less-expensive workers would, so long as the dollars currently paid to physicians are also transferred, allow maintenance of present levels of service with fewer dollars. Savings could allow development of some of the support models which are considered essential to community-based treatment of the chronically mentally ill (*A New Framework for Support for People with Serious Mental Health Problems*, Canadian Mental Health Association, 1993).

There are Canadian experiences which demonstrate the ability of nonphysicians to deal with severe mental ill health. In the Greater Vancouver Mental Health Service the crisis intervention teams are composed of nurses and social workers with psychiatrists, psychologists and police in back up roles. These crisis intervention teams deal with clients whose problems are more acute and difficult to handle than those seen by the many psychiatrists whose clientele consists entirely, or almost entirely, of families and individuals in stressful situations but without psychotic disorders.

In the United States there are psychiatric nurses trained at the master's level, and there are subspecialties in children's mental health, psychogeriatrics and community mental health nursing. The quality of care provided by these nurses has been established. (McFarland, G.K., and M.D. Thomas, *Psychiatric Mental Health Nursing*, 1991, Ch. 55.)

The professions who provide mental health services do not practice on a level playing field. Physicians are financially and legally favoured. Psychotherapy and counselling services provided by physicians are covered in all provincial medicare plans, whereas the same services provided by social workers, psychologists and trained counsellors are not. Services of these other providers are available at public expense only if the provider is paid by a hospital or some other publicly financed agency. Physician advantage is increased by the fact that only physicians can prescribe a variety of pharmaceutical and other treatments. Greater use of nonphysicians in mental health services will require an elimination of legal and financial barriers.

Consumers are likely to quickly accept a reduced role for physicians in the provision of mental health services. A study found that depressed elderly persons often sought no help but usually preferred physicians when help was sought. Social workers were their second choice. Preferences changed rapidly, however, if clinical nurse specialists with mental health training were available. It seems likely that nurses are not thought of as providers of mental health services merely because they have not historically been a source of these services. (Badger, T.A., "Mental Health Care for Depressed Older Adults", *App Nurs Res.*, August 1994, pp. 144-146.)

The 1990 Ontario Health Survey documented what kinds of professionals were visited by persons with mental health problems. Physicians were most commonly the source of assistance, but 22% of the 509,000 persons using mental health care consulted a social worker and 12% a psychologist. (*Mental Health in Ontario, The Ontario Mental Health Foundation Report to the Ministry of Health*, 1994, p. 37.) This level of utilization suggests a high degree of user acceptance of social workers and psychologists, an acceptance which is quite remarkable in light of the exclusion of these providers from medicare.

Other professionals could, with additional training, assume greater responsibility for care of the psychiatrically ill. From 1976 to the late 1980s, the number of psychiatric residents at the Montreal Children's Hospital fell from four to either one or none. The duties of the residents were largely assumed by nurses, and the transfer was not always successful. Many of the nurses were uncomfortable in their new roles. They felt unprepared for their new responsibilities on the wards and unable to competently provide on call advice to parents on the weekends when children were at home. The model was successful when nurses were prepared for their new roles. (Sterling, J., and J. Milne-Smith, "Breakpoints and Continuities: A Case Study of reactive change", *Nursing Administration Quarterly*, Spring 1994.)

Mental and psychological problems will be dealt with more cost-effectively when the capabilities of psychologists, clinical nurse specialists/psychiatric nurses, medical social workers and others are more fully utilized. Psychiatrists should be utilized only in special situations, and the role of family physicians should be reduced.

There are enough medical social workers, clinical psychologists, psychiatric nurses and other trained counsellors to allow a major transfer of functions to them, and their supply could be quickly expanded.

Neonatal intensive care

The neonatal intensive care unit (ICU) is a highly specialized setting in which many high-risk infants have similar problems and treatments, but in which every infant requires large amounts of individualized and sophisticated care and evaluation. The status of each infant is monitored constantly through both observation and laboratory and other testing. The monitoring and testing, and the changes in care which are needed, are now often the responsibility of a specialist nurse. The requirement for personnel with these special skills is likely to grow rather than shrink, and the work is quite unlike that in other health care settings. These service characteristics are well suited to extensive use of clinical nurse specialists.

Neonatal intensive care units tend to be found only in large teaching hospitals. In the past, pediatric specialists in training (pediatric residents) were responsible for much of the day-to-day and hour-to-hour decision making in neonatal ICUs. The number of medical residents has fallen considerably and a great deal of the care and decision making which were formerly the responsibility of the medical residents are now the responsibility of nurses.

Universities and hospitals offer courses in neonatal intensive care nursing. Such a course has been available since 1980 at the University of Alberta hospitals in Edmonton. In 1988, a 15-month program was begun at McMaster University in Hamilton. This program, which includes clinical and academic preparation, leads to a Master of Health Sciences. All applicants must have a BScN and at least two years of level three experience in neonatal intensive care. The graduates from the McMaster program call themselves Clinical Nurse Specialists/Nurse Practitioners (CNS/NPs).

Some of the McMaster graduates work in the Neonatal Intensive Care Unit (NICU) at The Hospital For Sick Children in Toronto. Seventy per cent of their time is spent on clinical duties including assessment, design of care plans, writing orders, prescribing medications, providing care and preparing for discharge. The remaining 30% of their time is spent in teaching and research (personal communication from Marilyn Ballantyne CNS/NP, July 12, 1994).

Formal training plus a legally expanded scope of practice for neonatal intensive care specialist nurses should, in the near future, lead to reduced expenditures on physician services. Physicians should be used as consultants rather than have primary and continuous responsibility for infants in Neonatal Intensive Care Units.

Nephrology

Renal dialysis is performed primarily by specialized nurses and technicians. Both work under the direction of nephrologists.

Clinical nurse specialists are now being trained at the masters level for the delivery of dialysis services.

Competition between registered nurses and dialysis technicians may increase. At the Montreal General Hospital, dialysis technicians have replaced nurses on the dialysis unit. At the Royal Victoria Hospital, the dialysis unit is staffed by nurses. Unit costs are lowest in the dialysis unit staffed by technicians. When these two hospitals merge, nurses and technicians will compete for continued employment.

There is, however, a third option. Clinical nurse specialists/nurse practitioners could become the primary decision makers in dialysis units. These nurses could, for the handling of most dialysis cases, assume the current functions of physicians. The units would be staffed by a mix of nurses and technicians, with nephrologists being involved only when a consultation is requested by the clinical specialist nurse. The use of the lower-cost technicians as major deliverers of care would be preserved and there would be less use of the most expensive providers (the nephrologists). Because the nurses and technicians are already fully involved in care, an expansion of the nurse roles would be unlikely to add significantly to costs per case. Payments to physicians would fall.

Hospitals wishing to spend less on dialysis without loss of quality should ask that statutes and/or regulations be changed to give specialist nurses the authority to order investigative procedures, interpret laboratory results, revise therapy, prescribe prescription drugs and admit and discharge dialysis patients.

Occupational Health

The evolution of occupational health nurses is an example of imaginative and sensible opportunism. Employers and compensation agencies needed personnel to evaluate, monitor and improve the safety of the workplace and coordinate rehabilitation of injured workers, and nurses moved into these roles.

The duties performed by occupational health nurses are not considered to be "medical care" and therefore can be performed within existing nursing legislation and without delegation from a physician. The nurses work as either salaried employees or as independent contractors or consultants. They may advise employers on workplace health hazards and/or act as case managers in the evaluation and rehabilitation of injured workers. Similar functions are served by some public health inspectors and by some union representatives, but the position of nurses in this field appears to be secure. Protection and consolidation of this role has been helped by the recognition of occupational health nurses as a specialist group and by their involvement in the Association of Rehabilitation Counsellors.

The ability of occupational health nurses to function without objections from physicians is more accidental than logical. The decisions that they make are often clinical and could easily have been seen by physicians as medical care. Presumably physicians did not have an interest in the field of occupational health and the emergence of independent nurses was therefore uncontested.

The success of occupational nurses in situations requiring constant application of clinical knowledge supports the general proposition that nurses with specialized skills should be performing many more functions than is usually now legally possible.

Oncology

Oncology is a field which has not been attractive to young Canadian physicians. Canada often has gone abroad for physicians to staff its cancer units.

The involvement of nurses in cancer treatment has increased in recent years, but physicians remain responsible for treatment decisions. Many of these treatment decisions are largely determined by the use of formulas and protocols. A situation in which relatively similar treatment is delivered to many patients is a situation in which it is very likely that more responsibility could be given to nurses and others, sometimes after additional training or experience. Replacement of some physicians by specialized nurses would reduce the need to recruit foreign physicians, would utilize the competencies of the nurses and would lower costs.

Nurses are the principal workers in the provincial Breast Screening Programs in Ontario and Manitoba. The nurses conduct the clinical breast examinations in association with a mammogram. This medical service is delivered by physicians in other provinces.

Ophthalmology

Issues related to the care and diagnosis of disorders of the eyes include whether the scope of practice of optometrists should expand, whether refractions should be performed by family physicians, the extent to which competition between ophthalmologists and optometrists should or can be encouraged, the role of optical technicians, whether it is ethical to both prescribe and sell glasses and whether there is a place in ophthalmology for clinical specialist nurses.

The Canadian Ophthalmological Society has for many years reported a shortage of ophthalmologists in Canada, with the shortage being seen as more acute in some provinces and regions than others.

The current supply of ophthalmologists would, however, be quite adequate (and perhaps excessive) if services were delivered differently. Substitution could occur through expanded roles for optometrists or for other providers such as clinical specialist nurses.

The current supply of ophthalmologists would be quite adequate if they gave first attention to eye care which can legally only be delivered by them. Many ophthalmologists spend a considerable part of their working day doing refractions, a service which can quite adequately, and often at lower cost, be provided by optometrists.

The optometrist supply is growing steadily. If a government should decide to pay for refractions only when done by an optometrist there are almost surely enough optometrists to provide all necessary services.

In about half of the states in the United States, optometrists are allowed to treat a variety of eye conditions. Optometry schools in the United States have for many years taught courses on the treatment of common eye conditions, and the School of Optometry at the University of Waterloo has, as of 1993/94, offered such a course.

In most provinces, changes in provincial legislation would be necessary to allow optometrists to treat common eye disorders and order necessary laboratory and other investigations. In Ontario, the Optometry Act allows optometrists to treat diseases listed in the regulations, but to date this list of diseases has not been prepared.

The extent to which expanded optometrist roles would alter health care costs is not known. Cost savings might be small. Optometrists are paid by fee-for-service. Their fee for a refraction is similar to that of a physician, and fee-for-service brings incentives for overservicing.

It is unclear whether or not there is a role for clinical nurse specialists in ophthalmology. There certainly is no need for another professional able to perform testing for glasses. Specialist ophthalmological nurses would improve the cost-effectiveness of health care if they were trained to perform high-volume procedures such as cataract surgery.

The increasing number of family physicians who test eyes for glasses may be a cause for concern. Medical schools teach very little if anything about this procedure, and a family physician who performs them is likely to have had minimal training. In the presence of an excess of other more highly trained professionals whose fees are no higher than those of a family physician, it may be reasonable to limit the opportunities for family physicians to perform refractions.

Orthopedics

Physiotherapists, orthopedic nurses or other providers could be trained to be fully responsible for a broad range of orthopedic care including common fractures such as those of fingers, toes, forearms and collar bones. These professionals could screen (triage) patients with orthopedic problems and refer only the more complex and difficult cases to specialist physicians.

There is a reported lengthening of the waiting time for an orthopedic consultation in the office and for hospital surgery. (S.D. Patterson MD, *Dialogue*, CPSO, January 1995, p. 7.) It is reasonable to search for ways to transfer funds and patients from orthopedic surgeons to other professionals so that specialist time will be spent only on those services which cannot be performed by other professionals. With transfer of both services and funds from orthopedic surgeons to other professionals there could be better patient access to orthopedic care and more services per dollar spent.

Palliative care

Palliative care is provided in hospital and in the community. It is provided by physicians, nurses, auxiliary nursing personnel, family and friends. Care at home is preferred by many patients and is becoming more necessary as the supply of hospital beds is reduced.

Palliative care nurses already have knowledge of the equipment and caring which can make dying in the community an acceptable and tolerable option. A full spectrum of palliative care could be provided by a nursing team which includes some specialist nurses able to order diagnostic tests and prescription drugs, including those necessary for pain control. Physician consultations would be asked for as needed. Such an arrangement would be simpler and more understandable to the patient and family, and it would be less expensive. Payments to physicians for palliative care would fall. The savings could, and should, be removed from the physician global payment fund and used to improve services to terminally ill patients.

Pediatrics

Nurses (public health nurses, nurse practitioners and others) have fully established their role in child health, including community neonatal care, immunization, poison control, breast feeding, oral rehydration, school health programs, the improvement of parenting skills, prevention of teenage pregnancies, caring for street kids, care and control of infectious diseases and a variety of other diagnostic, treatment and health promotion activities. Nurses are the dominant providers of community care, and it would be reasonable to legally recognize their leadership.

In addition to the established roles in primary pediatric care, clinical nurse specialists/nurse practitioners are now establishing their role in secondary and tertiary care. Neonatal intensive care nurses have demonstrated their ability to provide care of a highly specialized nature and to a highly vulnerable pediatric population (see earlier section).

The adequacy of pediatric nurse specialists as providers of primary medical care to children was demonstrated decades ago in Colorado. In more recent years, nurse practitioners working in many settings have shown their ability to provide primary pediatric care. The inability of these practitioners to prescribe medication and order investigations has been an impediment to their optimal use.

Prescribing pharmaceuticals

In 1993, at least 21 states in the United States had granted at least mid-level prescribing privileges to nurse practitioners. In 15 of these states the nurse practitioner privileges included the prescribing of controlled substances.

A recent New Zealand discussion paper, "Prescribing Rights in New Zealand", recommended the granting of prescribing privileges to more health care professionals. Advantages identified included more consumer choice, more complete care by the first contact person chosen by the patient and more complete care by the many community health care workers who look after persons with chronic disabilities. (*International Nursing Review*, November/December 1994, p. 168; *Nursing New Zealand*, September 1994.)

In 1994, a number of British District Health Authorities began experimenting with nurse prescribers. The nurses are allowed to prescribe the drugs listed in a Nurse Prescribers Formulary (*Professional Nurse*, October 1994).

It appears likely (but not certain) that nurse practitioners in Ontario who meet specific criteria will be authorized to prescribe a limited number of prescription drugs. Physiotherapists, optometrists and other professionals are seeking similar powers. Paramedics, podiatrists, chiropodists and dentists in Ontario now have the authority to use selected drugs without prior physician approval.

Expansion of the number of health care professionals authorized to prescribe prescription drugs is inevitable. Hopefully this expansion will be combined with increased roles for pharmacists as pharmaceutical advisors.

Radiology (diagnostic) (See also Chapter 5)

Increased use of technologists for the interpretation of X-rays would be of value in emergency care. There is seldom a radiologist available outside of regular office hours, but a technologist is available if an X-ray is taken.

Besides expanded use of X-ray technologists, there should be a reevaluation of the role of radiologists in the reading of X-rays which have already been read by specialists such as orthopedic surgeons or neurosurgeons. Paying for a second opinion on these X-rays is a luxury which should be abandoned. Once again, hospitals would be the immediate beneficiaries. No additional fee is paid to physicians who read X-rays, ultrasounds or other images as part of the complete care of a patient.

Respirology and pulmonary function

The role of the respiratory therapist has expanded steadily. This expansion has been approved by physicians and controlled by them. The activities of respiratory therapists now include pulmonary function testing, cardiac stress testing and the maintenance of anesthesia equipment. How much the role of respiratory therapists should be expanded is unclear, but the ease with which they have become responsible for sophisticated decisions suggests that the question merits study.

Sexually transmitted diseases (STD)

STDs are usually treated in special clinics. Their treatment and prevention are relatively circumscribed. This is an ideal situation for replacement of physicians with nurses. Nurses who have worked in these clinics for a number of years have the necessary skills and judgment to make a broader range of decisions, but a few months of formal education might still be a reasonable prerequisite to independent practice. The majority of patients visiting STD clinics would not need to be seen by a physician if nurses had the authority to prescribe medication, order investigations and refer when indicated.

Surgery

Dozens of high-volume surgical procedures are simple, quite safe and easy to learn. Many of these procedures are not as sophisticated, difficult or stressful as many of the clinical functions which are now routinely performed by nurses in neonatal intensive care units, dialysis units, palliative care teams and emergency departments. It is not reasonable to have these procedures performed by our most expensive health care personnel.

In 1992/93, Saskatchewan physicians performed 5,180 D and Cs (dilatation and curettage) for about $70 per procedure and 1540 therapeutic abortions for an average cost of $115 per procedure (physician fees only). There were also 2,850 tubal ligations at $180 per procedure and 2,600 vasectomies at $135 per procedure, plus facility costs when the procedures were performed at a hospital. Similar volumes and costs apply to many other procedures such as joint injections, hemorrhoidectomies, tonsillectomies, carpal tunnel decompression, varicose vein removal or ligation, lymph node biopsies and endoscopic procedures, as well as to acting as a surgical assistant.

Wound management in the community now costs $1 billion a year in the United States, and most of this care is delivered by nurses. A study showed wound management was better when nurses had received formal training, and that nurse judgment regarding wound management was better than that of physicians. (Turner, J.G., E.L.Larson et al, "Consistency and cost of Home Wound Management by Contract Nurses", *Public Health Nursing*, October 1994, pp. 337-342.)

The ability of nurses and trained technicians to learn complex technical tasks has been demonstrated many times. When looking for places where the costs of health care might be lowered, surgical procedures deserve very early attention.

Urology

The competence of nurses in the treatment of incontinence has been established. (Sale, P.G., and J.F. Wyman, "Achievement of Goals Associated with Bladder Training by Older Incontinent Women",

Applied Nursing Research, May 1994, pp. 93-96.) The competence of nurses will be even greater when formal training programs are available. The cost-effectiveness of clinical specialist nurses will improve when they are able to authorize a broader range of investigations and treatments.

Cystoscopies and retrograde pyelograms could be competently and less expensively performed by professionals other than specialist physicians.

Summary

Role changes are everywhere and they will continue. All types of workers and patients have been affected, and all will continue to be affected.

As the roles of health care providers have changed in the past, the biggest winners have been the physician specialists. The biggest direct winners from now on should be nurses and payers. The biggest indirect winners will be all who benefit from the preservation of a reasonable level of access to publicly financed health care.

Expanding the roles of nurses and others should not be an ad hoc process. A number of clinical, financial and other criteria should be methodically applied to literally hundreds of patient care activities. Governments and regional leaders, rather than physicians, should be the dominant participants, although all affected parties should be involved in discussions.

CHAPTER 9

Policy Analysis: Evaluating the Policy Options

Chapter 9 discusses the processes (the policy analyses) through which Ministers, public servants, planners, administrators, providers, taxpayers and others decide which policies are best. The adequacy of the skills of those who represent the public in the policy analysis process often determines how well the health care system serves the public.

A summary of the environment of health care

The environment of health care was described in Chapter 2, but a summary is presented here because an examination of the environment is the first stage of policy analysis. (This stage is sometimes referred to as the "situation analysis" or "environmental scan".)

Policy analysts need to be sensitive to the economic, political, social, cultural, historical and legal environments of health care as well as to its internal environment.

The external environment of health care is very different from the environment of only a few years ago.

All social spending, or lack of it, is now understood to be important to the health of the community. If health care is funded too generously, that generosity endangers the benefits which could have come from other social spending. The opportunity costs associated with excessive spending on health care are very high.

Physician control of health care is decreasing. Power is being redistributed. Competition among health care professionals is increasing.

Public participation is a routine part of the development of public policy. Governments find it difficult to proceed with health care revisions unless the public supports them, and the public may not support revisions unless safety is thought to be assured and the rationale behind the revisions is understood. Public participation is occurring because it improves decisions, because it is the right thing to do and because it is politically necessary. The economic environment has become dominant. Governments are broke. Public debt is at almost unmanageable levels and still growing. Public expenditures on health care in Canada are falling, and reductions will continue. Capping of health care expenditures is the norm, and the capping will continue. Capping applies to ministries, health care sectors and programs (such as hospitals, public health services, mental health services or emergency services), individual agencies and institutions, total provincial payments to physicians and other provider groups and total payments to individual providers on fee-for-service. Capping of regional public expenditures on health care also may soon be common.

The amount which provinces allocate for payments to physicians on fee-for-service is shrinking. The gross incomes of physicians are falling. Provincial expenditures on physician's services will fall even faster if there is a major transfer of functions from physicians to other professionals.

In the near future, some physicians (in at least some provinces) will not be able to bill the provincial insurance plans. Physicians without a billing number will, if they stay in Canada, either bill patients or private insurance companies or work where a billing number is not needed (such as on salary in a community health centre).

New types of legislation will allow an increase in the number of health care professionals able to practice as independent practitioners. Some of these independent practitioners will be able to order prescription drugs, order diagnostic tests and refer patients to other professionals for consultation.

The evaluation of policy options

When writing public policy and implementing public programs there are almost always options. It is often not easy to identify the options which are available, and it may be even more difficult to be sure which option is best.

Identification and evaluation of options is the heart of policy analysis. Evaluation of options usually involves the use of judgment, values, information and science.

Deciding what to recommend or do is most difficult when there is a shortage of information. In this situation, both strategic and operational decisions may be based in judgment and values more than in information and science.

Good process results in the best possible evaluation of the options. Careful evaluation helps decision makers make the "best guess", and a "best guess" is often all that can be expected.

Factors considered during policy analysis may be legal, financial, organizational, cultural, historical or political. They may be pragmatic or philosophical.

The effects of some factors considered during policy analysis are immediate. Other effects are delayed. Effects can be negative (e.g., conflict, unemployment, confusion and litigation) or they can be positive (e.g., more teamwork, more employment, more equity and a gentler and more sensitive health care network). It is almost always difficult to decide how much weight to give to various factors and different effects, and it is routine for different people to give different weights to the various factors and outcomes.

Estimating the cost-effectiveness of changes in roles requires estimation of cost and estimation of benefit. How will costs change, and how will outcomes change, if different providers are used? To answer these two basic questions, a number of more specific topics must be explored.

The experience of other countries, institutions or programs will often be important. Have the changes which are being evaluated been tested in other jurisdictions? Is there evidence to suggest that a service or activity can or cannot be performed satisfactorily by different providers? Did the introduction of a new worker, or the expansion of the role of existing workers, lead to changes in outcomes and/or cost?

Analysts will study the financial implications of expanded roles for various health care professionals. The average cost of specific activities or services performed by different providers will be examined, as will information concerning the cost of total care during one episode of illness or injury, or during a period of time such as a year. (Comparing costs is discussed later in this chapter.)

Analysts will wish to know how money will be found to pay those professionals whose scope of practice is to be expanded. Ministries of Health and of Finance will not be impressed with lower unit costs if total expenditures on health care go up. If services can be offered by more than one type of provider (e.g., if nurses can provide services which are also provided by physicians), governments will be much more likely to transfer functions to the lowest cost provider if both total costs and unit costs go down.

Will the changes in roles affect the safety with which services are provided? Does the amount and nature of training of the providers who will have new roles appear to be adequate?

The degree of opposition and support among health care providers will be assessed. To what extent will the changes in roles increase or decrease cooperation among professionals? Will new workers, or existing workers in new roles, have the cooperation of dominant providers such as physicians? Will more specialized personnel be available and be cooperative when back-up or referral are needed? How vigorously will the development of new roles be opposed, and can the changes proceed if opposition is sustained? If roles are being assumed by less-trained personnel, will there be access to more skilled personnel when such access is needed?

There will be consideration of the ease and the adequacy with which the outcomes of the services being transferred to new providers can be monitored. Is it reasonable to expect the professional decisions made by the new providers to be at least as good as the decisions made in the past by other providers? How will the adequacy of these decisions be measured, and by whom?

Will the changes proposed increase or decrease the opportunities for the system to monitor and/or improve professional decision making?

The frequency with which a service is delivered can be important. It is usually more useful to reduce the average cost of high-volume activities than to reduce the average cost of low-volume activities.

Comparisons of the outcomes of similar care delivered by different workers and teams will often not have been made, but, if made, the findings should be examined. In the absence of field testing, transfer of functions to less-trained staff may seem risky, but experience indicates that transfer will be safe so long as reasonable judgment is used. Experience indicates that allowing medical or dental services to be provided by professionals other than physicians and dentists does not lead to a lowering of quality.

Professionals who are well served by the status quo may demand that no changes occur until the changes have been scientifically evaluated. These demands should usually be ignored. Changes favoured by physicians, and implemented through delegation of functions to other providers, have seldom been scientifically evaluated before implementation. Expert opinion was usually all that was considered to be necessary. Demands for extensive evaluation prior to the introduction of change can be merely a tactic to delay change.

The status quo has been regularly proven to be ineffective, inefficient and/or wasteful. New delivery arrangements should not be expected to be perfect. They only need to be better than what exists now. Changes should be introduced when they appear to be reasonable.

Effects on patients will be considered. Are the proposed changes acceptable to the users? Some professionals may claim, and may believe, that changes will not be acceptable to users, but history suggests this is seldom the case. User objections have seldom been an obstacle to change.

Will the changes increase or decrease the range of choices available to users? A recent Gallup Poll in the United States reported that over half of Americans would accept care from a Physician Assistant, a nurse practitioner or a registered nurse. (*Observer*, American College of Physicians, December 5, 1994, p. 6.) A New Brunswick survey reported that 88% of respondents supported a larger role for nurses in health care, and 65% said they would consider seeing a nurse for their regular check-up. (*The Canadian Nurse*, December 1995, p. 11.)

Will the changes primarily protect the public or will they primarily protect the providers? Will the changes increase or decrease public control over the system?

The ease with which changes can be implemented will be important. To what extent will it be necessary to write or amend statutes? Governments almost always have more laws to pass than they can pass in the legislative time available. They also may not wish to give the opposition a chance to debate and question sensitive legislation. Changes are much easier to implement if they do not require changes in legislation.

How will the proposed policy changes affect collective bargaining agreements? These agreements may not be important to long-term planning, but in the short term they can markedly affect the cost of change and the difficulties associated with it.

How vigorously will the workers whose roles are being considered for expansion support the changes? How actively, for example, will nurses and their associations support governments who wish nurses to provide services now being provided by specialist physicians? What is the power of the players who will support the change, versus those who will oppose it?

Is there an adequate supply of personnel who might perform the new roles? If nurses are being considered for new roles, neither supply nor skills are likely to a problem. There are many unemployed and underemployed nurses, and most of these nurses have special skills in some clinical field.

The relationship between different health care services will on occasion affect whether it is practical to transfer a function. Can an activity be easily or rationally separated from related activities? If cystoscopies, for example, are routinely an integral part of some more complex urological procedure, then it may be unwise to have the cystoscopy performed by someone who cannot proceed with the remainder of the procedure. If, however, cystoscopies are commonly the only procedure being performed (and this is the case), then it becomes reasonable to see if the provider can be someone who is less expensive than a physician.

Educational factors cannot be ignored. Will the education system be able to reasonably quickly produce new workers in the desirable numbers? Will existing educational programs be able to assist existing workers to obtain the necessary new skills? If a new health care worker is being created, will there be an acceptable pool of applicants? What will be the effect on costs of education? How many years or decades will it take to develop the new professionals or to develop necessary new skills in existing professionals?

Will the changes increase equity among those providers who are in competition?

The location at which the effects of change are felt may also need to be considered during policy analysis. The degree of opposition or support for change may vary depending on whether the change will occur in the community, a hospital, a fee-for-service clinic or office, a capitated clinic, a public health unit, an occupational health office, a community health centre or elsewhere.

When the issue of quality is considered, evidence from randomized clinical trials is most desirable. Change should not, however, be abandoned if these trials have not been conducted. Earlier chapters have identified many instances in which roles have changed and fears of inadequate quality have been unfounded, e.g., use of dental therapists in Saskatchewan, admissions to home care without referral from a physician and the use of nurses to triage and treat patients in emergency departments.

Because scientifically acceptable evaluation of the impact of change will often not have been done prior to implementation of the change, there should be ongoing analysis. There should routinely be ongoing evaluation of both the existing and the new health care delivery patterns. Surveys can be used to measure consumer satisfaction and other subjective consumer outcomes. Analyses of records can be used to examine patterns of professional decision making and to identify outcomes. The decisions of both the former and the new providers should be compared to decisions and actions recommended in clinical protocols. There can be monitoring of drug use, use of laboratory tests, patient follow-up, patient education, etc.

The importance of each of the many factors which should be examined during policy analysis will change from situation to situation. The relative importance of the factors will also be seen quite differently by different players. In general, however, unit cost for a service of acceptable quality (including both direct and indirect costs) and user preference are likely to be the most dominant considerations when deciding which services should be provided by which professionals. In selected situations, other features such as provider cooperation, collective bargaining agreements, the need for statutory changes and/or practical problems of implementation will be important.

A number of principles should, to the extent possible, be honoured as provinces assess the various ways in which the roles of health care providers might be changed. These principles are discussed in Chapter 10.

Comparing costs

In many situations, more than one health care professional is, or will soon be, competent to deliver the required services. In these situations, those who pay the bills ought to prefer the least expensive provider. Lower costs, without loss of benefit to the consumer, are attractive.

Because of the importance of cost, the costing of alternative approaches to the delivery of care should be done in ways which can be understood by all players and which serve public rather than parochial interests.

Costing may be of a single service, a group of related services, an episode of care or all of the care delivered to an individual or group over time.

Comparison of the cost of a particular service is easy when all providers are on fee-for-service, the service is well circumscribed and the care involves few, if any, secondary (generated) costs. Refractions (testing of eyes) are an example. In this case a comparison of the fees of ophthalmologists and optometrists provides a relatively valid comparison of unit costs.

Unfortunately, a simple comparison of fees, or of direct costs when providers are not on fee-for-service, seldom provides a satisfactory comparison of costs. A comparison of the direct costs of office visits provided by competing caregivers to similar patients, for example, tells us nothing about generated health care costs. These generated or secondary costs include tests ordered, hospital use, referrals to other providers and drugs prescribed. A simple comparison of the cost of office visits also gives no consideration to the number of visits per episode of illness or disability, or to the number of visits per person per month or year.

Different providers may provide or order quite different volumes of service for similar cases. These differences in volume may be more important in terms of total cost than are differences in the cost of an individual visit or service. One provider may see hypertensive patients only half as often as another provider (without changes in outcome), one may prescribe more drugs, or one may order more diagnostic tests.

The costs of care for equivalent episodes of illness or trauma can be compared. The comparison could be of chiropractors and orthopedic surgeons treating comparable cases of back pain, of social workers and psychiatrists providing counselling to dysfunctional families, or of family physicians, nurse practitioners and specialist physicians treating a case of tonsillitis. Costing should consider the cost of the caregivers (fees and/or salaries and related costs) and of generated services.

Comparisons of cost per case become more useful if one also compares the cost of care to total populations over a period of time, e.g., the cost of orthodontic services per year. The total cost of orthodontic services per 1000 population depends partly on how many persons are thought to need this type of care. Lower costs per case may merely hide the fact that services are being provided to persons with questionable need. This possibility exists with respect to many conditions and types of health care including such things as blood transfusions, home care, family counselling, acne therapy, hypertension, obesity, insomnia, endoscopy and annual physical examinations.

The most valid cost comparisons are those which examine all sources of cost associated with care of comparable populations over time. Social workers, psychologists, family physicians and psychiatrists, for example, all provide outpatient counselling and psychotherapy. Comparison is easy if all providers deliver the same volume of counselling sessions per case, if no provider uses group therapy, if counselling or psychotherapy sessions are of similar length, if no provider uses drugs or other adjunct therapy and no provider refers the patient to anyone else. But professionals use quite different approaches to care and provide different volumes of care. Counselling sessions can be of different lengths. There can be variations in the number of sessions per case, in the volume of referrals, in the use of group rather than individual therapy, in the amount of investigative testing and in the volume of adjunct therapies which is prescribed. Good cost comparisons require data on all of the above factors.

Differences in costs should be examined whether or not the effectiveness of the different patterns of care has been determined. In the social worker/psychologist/psychiatrist/family physician example described, it is customary to assume that all professionals are being equally useful to their clients. If usefulness is assumed to be equal, then cost comparisons can provide a basis for policy decisions.

For chronic illness it may be most useful to compare the cost of care per year.

When comparing the costs of different providers, education costs may also merit consideration. They will, however, usually be a minor factor.

Financial information is often scarce. It may be necessary to decide whether information such as provider incomes can be useful. If the comparison is only of incomes, then the incomes should be compared fairly. Are all incomes calculated before taxes and after expenses? Are all incomes adjusted to reflect pension and other benefits or costs? The Sandy Hill Community Health Centre in Ottawa calculated the hourly direct costs of various salaried professionals as follows:

Nurse	$35
Nurse practitioner/health promote	$38
Family physician	$84
Street health worker	$18

(Report to the Board of the CHC from the Health Services Advisory Committee, December 1994.)

The hourly costs of the four CHC professionals are sufficiently different to suggest that services which are being delivered by physicians and which can be delivered by the less-expensive providers should be assigned to them.

The question of generalists versus specialists

This question will come up frequently when human resource policies are being assessed.

Defining "generalist" and "specialist" is not easy. These terms mean different things at different times and places. A "general" internist may be called a generalist because he or she looks after patients with diabetes, arthritis, headaches, congestive heart failure and other medical (versus surgical) conditions. But this "generalist internist" is certainly a specialist when compared to a family physician. Similarly, an orthopedic surgeon who treats both children and adults is obviously a generalist when compared to a pediatric orthopedic surgeon, but a specialist when compared to a family physician. A nurse with no advanced training who has worked for 20 years in obstetrics is trained as a generalist but has, through experience, become a specialist.

The problems of definition are minor compared to the more central issue of deciding when to favour specialist workers and when to favour generalists.

Generalists (of any type) appear to be best suited for initial assessments. Generalists may be the best persons to select the specialists to whom referrals should be made.

Generalist case managers and advisors are particularly suited for the development of care plans for multiproblem individuals and families. These multiproblem clients usually require assessment by, or services from, a broad range of social and health care professionals and/or agencies. As the number of providers serving one individual or family increases, it becomes more and more desirable that a generalist coordinate care and communication and be the main point of contact for the patient.

Specialization can lead to fragmentation of care. It has at times led to no one being in charge. Multiple caregivers delivering care to the same patient increase the likelihood of disagreement among caregivers and increase the likelihood that the recipient of care will be confused. Multipurpose providers are most attractive when one provider can possess the skills and judgment required to meet at least most of the needs of a patient or family.

A balance should be sought between the need for specialists and the advantages of the multipurpose worker. Progress has been made towards this objective. Public health nurses now, in many communities, provide an introductory level of personal care, mental health services and psychosocial support as well as their traditional education and health promotion services. Educational and health promotion functions are now often performed by home care nurses who formerly provided only personal care. The functions of occupational health nurses may include elements of personal care as well as assessment of workplace safety and the education of workers and employers.

But there are limits to the feasible expansion of the roles of a public health nurse, a home care nurse, a family physician, an occupational health nurse or any other provider. At some point, further expansion of the range of services being provided by one professional serves neither the client, the payer nor the professionals involved.

The multipurpose (generalist) worker can easily be expected to deliver more than is possible. The needs of patients are often too complex to be met by one provider. Even after reducing the number of providers to a minimum, it will not be possible to avoid the use of specialists and of teams of providers.

It is uncommon for health care professionals to be able to become, or remain, competent in a broad range of diagnostic and treatment situations. Continuing competence in a particular clinical field requires ongoing use of the relevant skills and knowledge and regular opportunities for involvement in appropriate upgrading activities. The issue of retaining competence places limits on the concept of the multipurpose worker.

Summary

The wisdom with which new kinds of health care professionals are developed, and the wisdom with which the roles of existing professionals are changed, will depend largely on the skill with which policy options are evaluated. All players, including policy makers, users, payers, planners, administrators and providers, should be actively involved in examining the options.

The most important factors to be taken into consideration during policy analysis are usually the amount of societal benefit which will accrue from each public dollar spent and the degree of public acceptance of the changes being considered. When all the available public resources have been spent, will the health status of the total population have been improved as much as was possible with the resources available? When changes are introduced, will the public welcome them?

CHAPTER 10

What Provincial Governments Should Do

Provincial governments, usually through their Ministries of Health, should be the lead players in reforming the manner in which health care is delivered.

Most provincial governments have not, as yet, fully accepted responsibility for determining which professionals should deliver which health care services. Many still delegate this responsibility to the dominant professions, primarily physicians. Only Ontario has passed a law which gives this function to the Minister of Health.

Accepting responsibility for how health care providers are utilized is only the first step. Ministers of Health next must make decisions and then see that the decisions are implemented.

Many of the decisions which governments should make are discussed in earlier chapters. Chapter 10 looks primarily at the skills, knowledge, assets and principles which will help governments implement the decisions they choose.

Understand the change process

The health care field is full of good ideas, but good ideas are of no value unless they lead to useful change. A good idea is more likely to be implemented if the change process is understood.

Levin has described the change process as defreezing followed by change (movement) followed by refreezing. The process can also be described as having five steps: the development of dissatisfaction with the status quo; destabilization of the status quo; identification of alternatives; implementation of changes; and establishment of a new status quo. The actions most appropriate for those who are promoting change differ depending on which stage has been reached in the change process.

Different types of people are dominant at different stages in the process of change. Innovators promote dissatisfaction with the status quo and provide the ideas and the energy which destabilizes the status quo. Early adopters (who may also be the innovators) are practical people who take the ideas of the innovators and implement them, usually in limited ways. They are the agencies and individuals who prove that change is possible. The early adopters are gradually joined by the late adopters – the less adventurous but willing. These late converts provide the critical mass which brings momentum to the change and consolidates success. The last group to join are the laggards; the hesitant followers. They would rather join than fight, or they join because they routinely support the status quo and the changes have produced a new status quo. Throughout the process there are always the rejectors. The size of this group tends to shrink gradually, but some people never accept change and continue to pretend it hasn't happened.

At the moment, it is clear that different parts of health care are at quite different stages of change.

The proposal that a significant portion of the services currently provided by specialist physicians should be provided by other professionals is at the innovation or early adopter stage, as is the proposal that the global fund for physician payments should be reduced when services are transferred to other professionals. These ideas now need the open support of large numbers of providers and users. (Nurses have the numbers and the power to move these ideas forward, especially if they gain the support of user groups.)

Regional health care systems have gone through the process of change and are now the new status quo. The late adopters have joined the move to this new organizational form. In some jurisdictions, even the disinterested late followers are on board.

Decentralization of provincial health care responsibilities to the regional systems is underway but is not yet a new status quo.

Creation of a more level health care playing field is at different stages in different provinces. It is most advanced in Ontario because of the Regulated Health Professions Act, which eliminates control, by any profession, of the scope of practice of any other profession.

In Ontario, implementation of a more level playing field has clearly begun. In Ontario, nurses can now concentrate on convincing government that nurses should provide a broader range of health care services. In other provinces, nurses and other health care professionals must still work to escape from the medical model while also pursuing new roles.

Find, foster and protect allies

Changing the way health care is delivered requires provincial leadership, but the introduction of the changes will be more successful if the province has many allies. Provinces should seek, promote and welcome initiatives by, and support from, consumer groups, regional agencies, professions, hospitals, labour unions, community-based health care programs, municipal governments and everyone else. All of these agencies and interest groups can be helpful to governments wishing to implement less expensive ways to deliver high-quality health care.

To work with these many players requires flexible public servants. Bureaucrats who support the centralized top-down approach to health care evolution will either have to change or be moved out of the way.

Involvement of all major players in policy development will, at times, lead to modification of the strategies and even the goals of government, but the benefits can be substantial. Widespread involvement and support can bring better policies, better implementation of policies and more health care per dollar spent. The participative approach to policy selection is slow and demanding, but if well managed it brings allies. And allies allow change to be more orderly and more politically safe.

Consumers will not necessarily understand why there should be changes in the roles of health care providers. Consumers will be told by physicians, and told loudly, that their safety is being threatened. Governments – with the assistance of others who favour change – should, in a planned and ongoing manner, sponsor programs through which public opinions and advice can be received and the public informed of the rationale for change. The public is an essential ally.

The professionals whose functions are being expanded are natural allies of governments proposing change, but their support may need to be cultivated. The transfer of functions to specialist nurses from specialist physicians, for example, will be difficult if nursing leaders are not prepared to compete with physicians. If nursing leaders are hesitant to support new roles for nurses throughout health care, governments should actively seek their support. If this support cannot be obtained, governments can either pursue some other policy track or postpone action until the support of nurses is assured.

Governments are not likely to welcome confrontation with physicians, especially physician specialists, unless nurses and at least some of the public are on side. Governments may, if allies are not visible, prefer the second most attractive policy direction, namely the preparation of family physicians as mini-specialists.

Governments should not exclude physicians (or any other affected players) from discussions, but vested interests of any kind must be seen as such. Allies are essential, but there will be times when alliances are not possible. It should be taken for granted that physicians will oppose, obstruct, obfuscate, delay or use any other available tactic to preserve turf, income and power. The favoured tactic will often be to study, study and study, followed by pilot projects and reevaluation.

Allies may need to be sought within Ministries of Health as well as outside of them. Bureaucracies can be powerful opponents of change. Ministers must be certain that their senior staff can and will contribute to change, and senior staff must be certain that staff throughout the Ministry understand and accept change. If the intradepartmental milieu welcomes the emergence of innovators then innovators will emerge.

Remove policies which impede change

There are financial, legal, organizational and cultural obstructions to optimal use of health care professionals. Governments should provide leadership in the removal of most of these obstructions.

The Ontario Regulated Health Professions Act eliminated one legal obstruction to change. Physicians are, in Ontario, no longer legally able to determine the scope of practice of other professionals. All provinces should make this change.

The new Ontario statute is not perfect, but the principles are sound. The Ontario statute does not, for example, fully recognize the extent to which many health care professionals diagnose and treat, but it has created a legal environment in which it is easier to expand the roles of nurses and other health care professionals.

Pharmacy Acts may have to be altered to authorize the prescribing of pharmaceuticals by an expanded list of professionals. Medical Care Insurance Acts may have to be changed to allow payments to be made to professionals who have in the past been excluded. Hospital Acts may have to be changed to allow patients to be admitted by professionals other than physicians.

The Public Health Acts in most provinces impede the leveling of the public health playing field. All provinces should eliminate the requirement that public health units be headed by a physician.

Financial impediments to change may be enshrined in statutes, in regulations or in other forms of Ministry policy. Obstructive policies may affect who can be paid (often payments are made only to physicians) or where services may be provided as insured services (some services are covered only when provided in hospitals). The extent to which policy changes will require statutory changes varies from province to province.

Policies or agreements which limit the ability of government to transfer funds when functions are transferred are obstacles to optimal use of various providers. These obstacles to better spending were created by governments, and governments can eliminate them. Unless funds are able to be moved when functions are moved, financial forces may prevent the transfers of function. When midwives provide insured services, for example, provincial obstetrical costs increase unless the payments to the midwives are made from the global fund used to pay fee-for-service physicians.

Physicians have stated that expanded use of other health care professionals should not be financed with dollars which are currently paid to physicians. They do not wish midwives, chiropractors, clinical nurse specialists, optometrists, etc. to have access to any of the Ministry of Health dollars currently allocated for payments to physicians on fee-for-service. This physician wish is not realistic in light of shrinking public spending on health care and the large body of evidence which supports greater use of less-expensive health care providers.

The payment of physicians by fee-for-service inhibits use of other professionals. Payment by capitation or salary encourages transfer of functions to other professionals. Governments should continue their exploration of alternative physician payment methods.

Governments should eliminate discriminatory payment practices. Physicians are the only profession whose services are fully insured, and this is unfair and unwise when other professionals can provide many services at lower cost and sometimes at higher quality. As discussed earlier, policies prevent social workers, psychiatric nurses and psychologists from providing insured mental health services. This results in taxpayers often paying too much for counselling, psychotherapy and other services.

The way in which the scope of practice of professionals is described can contribute to high spending on health care. This is discussed at length in Chapter 1.

There are cultural impediments to change. Governments and the public are often unwilling to ignore the advice of physicians regarding the competency of other professionals. Hopefully there will, in the near future, be greater recognition of the extent to which physician decisions are often self-serving. It is time now to start allocating functions on the basis of what is in the public interest.

Hospital culture may also interfere with change. The hospital milieu is dominated by physicians, and other independent practitioners who wish to work in hospitals may have to contend with an unfriendly environment.

Incentives and disincentives

Those who promote new roles for less-expensive providers are more likely to find allies if the changes being promoted will bring benefits to the potential allies.

Incentives which encourage professionals to change include greater job security, more job satisfaction, more career options, higher income, greater prestige, greater personal and professional independence and more opportunities for career advancement. Disincentives include lower incomes, less job satisfaction, etc.

Non-financial rewards are important to many health care providers. The prospect of unemployment has made job security important. Professional freedom may also be seen as important. Because of the importance of these and other non-financial factors, it is likely that the roles of many workers can be significantly expanded without significant increases in their incomes.

In these times of acute fiscal restraint, governments should look for non-financial incentives to change. Workers who wish their roles to expand should place non-financial objectives ahead of a wish for major increases in income.

Maintain a competent public service

A number of recommendations have been made regarding what governments should do, but many of these things will not get done unless the skills of the bureaucrats are adequate. If the competence and leadership of provincial bureaucrats are inadequate, then regional agencies, health care institutions and programs, university faculties and professional associations may become the key players. But none of these players can fully compensate for inadequacies in provincial Ministries of Health.

It is the responsibility of the Deputy Minister of Health to be sure that specific public servants are assigned to the task of strategic thinking and planning. It is the responsibility of the deputy minister, the assistant deputy ministers and other senior members of the bureaucracy (including senior staff within the Minister's Office) to be sure that strategic tasks are continuously given attention. It is the responsibility of all senior staff to contribute to a ministry milieu in which creativity, openness, competence and an interest in the careful spending of public money are rewarded.

If policy and planning activities are poorly performed in any particular province, then it can only be hoped that other provinces will be the leaders. One of the great strengths of the Canadian constitutional division of powers is that any province can be an innovator.

Fund needed research

Evidence and logic fully justify industry-wide changes in the way various health care professionals are utilized. Exactly what the changes should be, however, is still often not clear.

Some changes in roles can with confidence be introduced immediately, but others need examination. Exactly what services should be provided by specialist clinical nurses, and where? How much will costs go down, and how many physicians will be displaced? What additional training is needed, and where will it be provided? How difficult will the various changes be? How many statutes and regulations require amendment?

These and many other questions need investigation by either staff within Ministries of Health or by outside experts. Governments, primarily provincial governments, should divert research and policy development resources to these questions.

Early attention should be given to the identification of areas of service where substitution is most feasible and will bring the greatest savings. Much of the needed information is in the files of the provincial medicare plans.

Some of the funds for needed research can be found by abandoning the kind of manpower studies which have traditionally been done. Such studies usually assume that utilization patterns in the future will be similar to those of the past. This is not a reasonable assumption. The number of physicians or other professionals who will be needed cannot be estimated with credibility unless role changes are anticipated.

Guiding principles

The preservation of a satisfactory and comprehensive publicly financed health care system depends on doing more with less. More cost-effective use of health care providers is one way to do more with less.

A number of principles and processes should guide policy analysts and public decision makers as they work to improve the way health care providers are utilized.

1. Statutes governing health care professionals should be rewritten to prevent any profession from having legal control over

the scope of practice of any other profession. Authority to amend the scope of practice of health care professionals should be vested in the Minister of Health or the Cabinet. Regulations which prevent professionals from delivering services which they can competently deliver serve no one except those who do not have to compete.

2. When services are transferred from one provider to another the dollars associated with the services should also be transferred. The transfer of services from physicians to nonphysicians should be associated with a decrease in total payments to physicians.

3. Services provided at public expense should be insured either only when performed by the lowest-cost provider or insured only to the level of the cost of provision by the lowest-cost provider.

4. Increased opportunities for nurses to provide primary care should not be ignored, but substitution of specialist nurses for specialist physicians should receive the greatest attention. Specialist clinical nurses should, as quickly as possible, deliver a significant minority of the services currently being delivered by specialist physicians. Earliest attention should be given to those services or service areas in which nurses have already established their competence (such as dialysis, neonatal intensive care, obstetrics, pediatrics, geriatrics, home care, palliative care, anesthesia and serving as surgical assistants) but there should also be early attention to high-volume surgical and diagnostic procedures.

5. Many professional decisions are less than ideal. This comment applies to the decisions of all professionals. When functions and decisions are transferred from one type of health care professional to another, the number of inappropriate decisions may not change. Regardless of which professionals deliver health care, there will be a need (as there is now) for routine monitoring of clinical decisions, and a continuing need for programs which help professionals improve their decisions (see many chapters in *Spending Smarter and Spending Less*; Sutherland and Fulton, 1994).

6. User fees can encourage use of the lowest-cost providers. Consumers who choose to obtain care from a high-cost provider should expect to be responsible for the additional cost.

7. The scope of practice of nurses should be defined in the same open-ended way as is used for physicians. The potential of nurses cannot be fully realized if their scope of practice is defined in a narrow way.

8. Legislation should authorize all independent professionals to establish diagnoses and to discuss those diagnoses with consumers.

9. All provinces should identify payment policies and laws which interfere with the cost-effective delivery of health care, and then develop plans for the elimination of these impediments to good spending.

   Payment policies should allow optimal use of the lowest-cost professionals. In mental health, for example, financial discrimination against appropriately trained and/or experienced social workers, psychologists, counsellors and nurses should end.

   All qualified mental health workers should have the same degree of opportunity to provide publicly insured mental health services. Regulations which authorize public payments to physicians and do not authorize public payments to other equally competent (or more competent) professionals who deliver the same services are discriminatory and not in the public interest.

10. Some X-ray technologists should, as quickly as possible, be trained to read those X-rays whose interpretation can be adequately taught in a 6 to 12 month training program.

11. There should be early major expansion of the use of pharmacists as advisors in the use of drugs. The expansion of this role is needed whether or not more professionals are given the authority to prescribe prescription drugs.

12. Expanded roles for nurses and other health care professionals usually should not be delayed pending extensive research and pilot projects. Decisions should follow the patterns established by physicians in their delegation of tasks to other workers. Alvin Toffler has said: "In dealing with the future, at least for the purposes at hand, it is more important to be imaginative and insightful than to be one hundred percent right" (as quoted by Dr. Helen Gordon, President, Ontario College of Physicians and Surgeons, *Dialogue*, March 1996).

13. Educational programs should constantly adapt as the roles of health care professionals change. In some cases, such as with clinical specialist nurse training programs, more resources will be needed. In other cases, such as with physician training programs, enrollments should continue to fall.

Summary

The primary challenge for governments, especially provincial governments, is to spend their limited supply of health care dollars as well as possible. One of the ways to increase cost-effectiveness is to lower labour costs. One of the ways to lower labour costs is to deliver services with less-expensive personnel.

Greater use of health care professionals other than physicians, and more equitable access by all professionals to the public dollars spent on health care, will create direct competition between physicians and other professionals. To take advantage of this competition, the zero-based budgeting principles should be applied, i.e., funds should be allocated in the way which brings greatest public benefit.

Physicians can justifiably expect to continue to provide many complex services and to have many of these services insured by provincial medicare plans. They cannot, however, expect to retain the current levels of protection of either income or clinical turf.

Financial, legal and other obstructions to optimal use of all types of health care professionals should be eliminated or at least substantially reduced.

CHAPTER 11

What Nurses Should Do

M uch of what nurses should do is already underway in some provinces, but some is not.

Terminology needs review. Nurses should describe themselves as "health care" providers more than as "nursing service" providers. How much of health care should be delivered by nurses is unclear, but it is clear that neither nurses nor the public are served well by never-ending discussion of whether a particular service is "nursing", "medical care", "chiropractics", "podiatry" or something else.

The concept that "a nurse is a nurse is a nurse" should be stored with other vestiges of Florence Nightingale. Individual nurses routinely have quite different visions, preferences and skills. These differences will increase and will be associated with increasingly diverse functions, needs and incomes. This diversity is inevitable and desirable. It should be seen as an asset. Failure to accept, nourish and adapt to the diversity among nurses will lead to internal conflicts and will reduce the ability of nurses to give attention to common interests.

Nurses should plan boldly and be proactive. Michael Decter, in his book *Saving Medicare* states:

> "Nursing organizations are going to have to be aggressive, not simply about opposing changes which they view as detrimental to their members, but in recommending constructive alternatives." (p. 118)

Michael Decter is right, but the recommendations must be detailed and credible as well as constructive. Each recommendation must be supported by a realistic and competent (rather than vague and wishful) explanation of how it might be implemented.

Recommendations or proposals must acknowledge government agendas, acknowledge the priorities of users and acknowledge impediments to implementation.

Nurses will often need to look outside their profession for assistance in preparing the needed working papers, reports and explanations. They may benefit from outside advice on matters of economics, labour negotiations, lobbying, policy development, dealing with government and consensus seeking. Most nurses have an academic and practical expertise in only one field – the delivery of health care. If patients and communities are to benefit fully from the expertise of nurses, then nurses must learn to fully use the skills of other kinds of experts. The CNA has a communications department headed by someone with a background in communication – not nursing. This model should be copied. It is not a betrayal of nurses, it is a strengthening of them.

During the Manitoba 1995 provincial election, the Manitoba nurses used television and newspaper advertisements to advocate greater use of nurses to perform some tasks now largely performed by physicians. The goal is commendable, but the strategy was not sufficiently complex or sustained. If there are to be new career options for nurses, the theme of new roles must be continuously promoted and be expressed with logic, options, practicality and specifics. Bureaucrats and politicians cannot be expected to support ideas which bring new costs or which do not appear to be sensible and possible.

Nurses should be aware of the many factors which will affect the success with which they identify and/or satisfy their objectives (Figure 11.1).

Nurses should give more attention to competence and expanded roles than to advanced academic qualifications. They should be more intent on the development of specialist skills in large numbers of nurses than on having a small number of specialist nurses with masters degrees or PhDs.

There will never be enough resources for nurses to pursue all of their goals and objectives, and therefore the goals and objectives must be ranked so that resources can be allocated first to those with the highest ranking. Expansion of the legal scope of practice of nurses with advanced training should be high on the list.

The fusion of diploma and baccalaureate nursing programs has progressed well, with collaborative projects in place in all provinces (Goldenberg, G., W. Gerhard, A. McFadden and E. Johnston, "Collaboration in nursing education", *The Canadian Nurse*, January 1995), but this exercise continues to consume scarce resources. The move towards baccalaureate training for all nurses should be accelerated and simplified, especially in Ontario.

Figure 11.1

Factors Affecting the Success of Nurses

Internal Factors (factors within nursing)
Clarity of goals and objectives
Priorities chosen
Mindsets/perceptions/assumptions concerning
- ability to compete
- willingness to compete
- the worth of outside advice
- caring versus curing
- the way physicians and their services are perceived
Wealth
Willingness to spend
Skills (of nurses and their advisors), including;
- internal consensus seeking
- alliance building
- communication and selling of preferences
- identifying and seizing windows of opportunity
- choosing priorities which are consistent with public priorities, sensitive to the priorities of others, and compatible with reality
- building, and working within, collaborative health care delivery
Knowledge (of nurses and their advisors) of:
- the policy development process
- the planning process
- how governments work
- relevant legislation
- the goals of other players
- the strengths and weaknesses of other players
- the lobbying process
- experience elsewhere
- sources of power and how to increase it

External Factors
The agendas of provincial governments
The legislation in place
The economic crunch
The power of opponents
The objectives of opponents
The skills of opponents
Social priorities
Public perceptions
The slowness of statutory change

The goals and objectives selected by nursing will be more attainable if specific strategies are developed for each goal and objective.

A strategy designed to consolidate the current position of nursing, for example, would seek to protect nursing from loss of functions to other professionals and would encourage the identification of "nursing" functions as functions which should not be able to be legally provided by other workers. Preservation would be the objective and protectionism the strategy. (This objective is a non-starter. "Nursing" cannot be defined and it cannot be protected from provision by others. Circling the wagons at this moment in time is not in the best interests of either nurses or the public.)

If nurses seek expansion of their roles in primary care, the chosen strategies would demonstrate the competence of nurses in these roles, seek elimination of statutory and regulatory impediments to nurses playing these roles, demonstrate the financial advantages of role expansion, identify funding options which do not increase the total costs of health care and seek public support. Nurses in most provinces have demonstrated their eagerness for expanded roles in primary care and health promotion, but their strategic plans tend to be deficient. Insufficient attention has been given to legal and financial impediments to change and to questions of the breadth and depth of nurse competence.

If nurses seek expanded roles in secondary and tertiary care, the strategies will be similar to those described in the preceding paragraph, but with at least one significant difference. Competing with specialist physicians will occur on as many fronts as there are physician specialties, and strategies and tactics will vary with the specialties involved.

Strategies become easier to develop as goals and objectives become more specific. If, for example, nurses wish to be the professionals who are recognized as being best suited for most geriatric assessments and for development of most geriatric care plans, then strategies will be directed to alteration of the policies, funding, care delivery and evaluative mechanisms in long-term care. If nurses wish to become the dominant professionals in public health, they should work for elimination of the current statutory protection of Medical Officers of Health. Nursing in public health cannot fully emerge unless nurses are legally able to be the Chief Executive Officers of public health units.

There are dozens of goals and objectives which nurses might choose to pursue. Many of these will, hopefully, relate to expanded roles for nurses in the delivery of secondary and tertiary health care.

Nurses should be aware of, and highly sensitive to, the political and economic climate of their province. They should know the mood and personal objectives of their Premier and Minister of Health. Nurses could offer no-cost seminars and workshops to politicians and senior bureaucrats. These workshops are expensive, but, if well done, they can acquaint decision makers with information and promote options central to the objectives of nurses.

Although nurses are a powerful group, they will be most successful in attaining their goals if they find allies.

Nurses, for example, have interests in common with pharmacists. These common interests could be the basis for joint actions. Pharmacists wish an expanded role as advisors on drug utilization and on the monitoring of drug use, and some nurses wish to have drug prescribing authority. The search by nurses for prescribing authority will become more defensible if it is known that they wish pharmacists to be their pharmaceutical advisors. Nurses will feel more secure as prescribers if they lean heavily on pharmacists for advice, and the role of pharmacists in "pharmaceutical care" will be strengthened if nurse prescribers routinely look to pharmacists for advice. The move of pharmacists away from products and towards patients will be strengthened. The objectives of both professions will be supported by an alliance.

The support of the public for expanded roles for nurses should be actively pursued. The public already thinks highly of nurses, but support for new roles will be more assured if nurses implement a program of regular contact with seniors organizations, service clubs, religious groups, educational organizations, community associations and other similar groups.

If nurses seek public support for expanded roles for themselves in primary, secondary and tertiary care, the public will (quite understandably) see nurses as wanting to become doctors. How will nurses respond? Some nursing leaders are vehemently opposed to being seen as mini-doctors. Will nurses waste energy and resources on terminological arguments? The option is to promote public discussion of the broad range of health care which is already being delivered by nurses, and of how nurses could play an even greater role.

The search for allies should not be conducted only by umbrella nursing organizations such as provincial or national nurse associations. Alliances should also be built within communities and regions. They can be between nurses and a variety of groups and agencies, or between groups of nurses in a particular region or community.

Physician associations and Colleges will seldom be allies, but nurses should welcome support from individual physicians or physician groups (such as physicians in community health centres).

Be willing to compete

Nurses know that physicians will oppose many of the changes which nurses support. Unfortunately, many nurses feel that they cannot compete with physicians. Others do not wish to do so. "Competing" is seen as unprofessional and not in keeping with the traditions of nursing.

If nurses choose not to compete, then governments may either continue with the status quo or promote changes which do not require the support of nurses. If nurses do choose to compete, they can – assuming they are willing to use the resources available – do so with success.

To compete, nurses must be willing to spend money – lots of it. The competition is well organized and well financed. The two physician organizations in Ontario have a combined operating budget of about $60 million per year. Significant parts of these budgets are spent on the lobbying, report writing, committee work, etc., which is a prerequisite to being a major player in health care policy development.

Major players such as physicians dominate partly because they are historically and emotionally prepared for dominance, but partly because they spend freely. Money is no substitute for thought, courage, planning and leadership, but it is a useful adjunct to all of those. Change agents tend to be more successful when there is adequate funding of research, travel, consultants, think tanks, lobbying, policy papers, consensus building and the preparation of plans.

Nurses must convince provincial governments that the cost-effectiveness of health care will increase if there is redirection to nurses and other professionals of some of the current payments to physicians. This is a threatening and competitive proposition which will quickly bring a vigorous response from physicians.

Health care dollars are distributed partly on the basis of evidence and public wish, but distribution may also be consistent with old adages such as "them that has, gets", and "the squeaking wheel gets the grease". One could also say that "the meek" do not inherit the health care dollars. Are nurses willing to sign on for a long and expensive war?

Nurses who are interested in expansion into service areas currently reserved for physicians should recognize the tactical importance of the agreements which exist in most provinces between the Ministries of Health and the provincial medical associations. These agreements often give physicians special access to the policy-making process and provide guarantees regarding expenditures on physicians services. Nurses need a strategy for amendment of these agreements and for assurances that nurses will have equal access to government.

Competing may require lobbying. The success of lobbying depends on the message, the messenger, the manner in which the message is delivered, who it is delivered to and when it is delivered. Messages should be sensitive to the goals and values of the recipients, should be delivered through a messenger who is acceptable to the recipient, should be delivered to persons who are able to influence the final decision, should transmit an element of flexibility, should be well documented but concise and should be free of personal or other abuse. Messages should be delivered early and often. Decisions are usually easiest to influence before they have been firmly made.

The extent to which nurse roles will expand will often depend on the financial impact of change. How much can or will provinces pay specialist nurses? The steering committee which made recommendations to the Ontario government regarding nurse practitioners recommended a salary of $60,000 to $80,000. Midwives in Ontario (who will not always also be nurses) will be paid about $55,000 per year as a starting salary. What pay scale will be acceptable to nurses with specialist skills? What will taxpayers be prepared to support? At what income levels do nurses cease to be more cost-effective than other providers?

Changes in roles should not increase public spending on health care. If nurse practitioners, clinical nurse specialists, physiotherapists, etc., see expanded roles primarily as a way to increase income, or if they ask that new health care money be found to pay for their expanded roles, then the expanded roles are less likely to materialize. If income expectations are reasonable, and if nurses and others ask that physician dollars be transferred as functions are transferred, then governments will be more interested in change.

The importance of timing

Windows of opportunity may arrive unexpectedly. In 1994, the Ontario Ministry of Health announced $18 million would be spent improving community mental health services in preparation for the closing of beds in psychiatric hospitals. Regions were asked to prepare plans for use of this $18 million. This was an opportunity for nurse and social worker organizations to aggressively offer resources and funds to help prepare these regional plans and, in the process, assure dominant roles for nurses and social workers in the community mental health service networks.

The year or two prior to the termination of an agreement between a province and its physicians is a window of opportunity. It is prior to the termination of these agreements that nurses and others should define the changes which they wish to see in the next agreement. If the changes desired need statutory amendments, such amendments can take several years. When the next long-term agreement between the Ministry and the provincial medical association has been signed the window of opportunity may be temporarily closed.

Reductions in the number of physicians in specialty training programs offered opportunities for nurses and others to fill a void. (This opportunity may have been narrowed by a recent lengthening of the mandatory years of physician post-graduate training prior to licensing, but opportunities still exist.) The Ontario government has, in its selection of the areas into which nurse practitioners should eventually move, recognized the opportunities created by reductions in specialty training positions for physicians.

The 1996 announcement that Ontario would experiment with capitation as the method of payment for all physicians providing primary care in selected communities is a window of opportunity. Nurses will need to move quickly if they are to strengthen their roles in the provision of primary care.

Summary

Nurses should revise their perceptions (including their self-image) and their expectations, and improve their ability to accomplish what is wanted.

Nurses should clarify and broaden their objectives. These objectives should be founded on full recognition of the potential for independent roles for nurses in secondary and tertiary care as well as in primary care. In preparation for expanded roles for a large number of nurses, and in many types of care, high priority should be given to the preparation of nurses with specialist skills.

Flexibility is important. Different provinces will choose to proceed in different ways and at different speeds. Nursing will achieve its greatest gains if attention is focused on those provinces which offer the most fertile ground for change, and if changes proposed acknowledge the special characteristics of the province concerned. Proposals for change must be customized to the statutes and history of each province.

CHAPTER 12

The End

This book has set out some of the ways in which the roles of health care professionals might change, some of the obstacles to change, and some of the ways in which the obstacles might be overcome.

The policy options available are many and varied. The rate at which changes may occur, and the processes through which the changes may occur, are equally varied.

With changes in who delivers health care, and who has the authority to order it, Canadians can receive more health care per dollar spent. Only two things are needed and both are possible.

First, the professional who can deliver care most cost-effectively must be identified. Sometimes this identification will be easy, sometimes it will not. Sometimes decisions will be made on the basis of judgment, sometimes on the basis of evidence, and most often on the basis of both.

Secondly, legislation and policies must be altered so that the preferred providers become the actual providers. The professional who is thought to be able to deliver a service most cost-effectively must become the provider of that service. Laws, payment patterns and other impediments to rationalization of the system must be removed.

If these changes are not made, Canadians will continue to pay more for many services than they should be paying.

Too many health care services are legally able to be delivered only by physicians. Too many services which can be provided competently by more than one type of professional are paid for by government only if provided by physicians.

Too much care which could be delivered by other professionals is being delivered by specialist physicians, and the gap between generalist and specialist caregivers is widening. It will continue to widen unless steps are taken to reverse the trend.

Most services can be competently provided by more than one type of professional. Unfortunately, Canada (all provinces) has developed patterns of law and of payment which have prevented full utilization of the skills and knowledge of almost every professional except physicians.

If nurses are creative and aggressive they may be the major beneficiaries of the changes which will occur. If they are slow and timid, they may lose major areas of health care to both existing professionals and to new professionals who will emerge.

Physicians are the professional group most likely to have significant areas of activity transferred to other professionals, with specialist physicians being more at risk than family physicians.

Progress towards the preferred future will be most successful if there is a good understanding of the factors which will affect or determine what will happen. These factors include the willingness of governments to disturb the status quo, the quality of the evidence supporting changes in roles, the attitudes and objectives of the professions (but especially nurses), the political skills and courage of each profession (but especially nurses), the willingness of physicians to accept lower incomes, the volume of out-migration of physicians as the changes are being discussed, and the response of the public to the changes.

When considering whether or not a particular professional should be allowed to provide a particular health service, it will be wise to remember both how often physicians have transferred functions to other providers and why these transfers have or have not occurred. The delegation of functions by physicians to other workers has usually been made quickly and without prior scientific evaluation when that delegation has been in the best interests of the physicians. The changes have seldom been made if they have been a threat to the incomes of physicians or if they disturbed the position of the physician at the top of the medical care team.

Transfers of function have been readily accepted when they served the objectives of physicians. Such transfers should now be equally readily accepted when they serve the public interest.

As other professionals seek to replace physicians in both primary and specialist areas of service, physicians will claim that patients are being put at risk. Such cautionary notes will always be in order, but they should not be accepted unless they have been examined and found valid.

The extent to which nurses and other professionals have replaced, and will increasingly replace, physicians is not yet fully appreciated by physicians. A report by a Task Force of the College of Family Physicians of Canada and the Royal College of Physicians and Surgeons of Canada recommends that "primary medical care be provided by family physicians working with other professionals and that secondary and tertiary care be provided by specialists/consultants." (*The Relationship between Family Physicians and Specialists/consultants in the Provision of Patient Care*, 1993.) In the future, this sentence will be rewritten (by different authors) to recommend "that primary, secondary and tertiary health care be provided by many different and independent health care professionals."

Health care has for a decade or more been demanding greater productivity from everyone. Many professionals, especially nurses in institutions, find work extremely stressful as staff numbers per patient shrink but workload per patient grows. One way to decrease the stress of many caregivers on the wards and in the community is to transfer duties (and their associated funding) to less-expensive personnel.

This book has explored ways in which payers, in particular provinces, can reduce the extent to which our most-expensive health care providers deliver services which could be adequately delivered by less-expensive personnel. From the point of view of the payers and the users, the preferred option is a marked expansion in the use of nurses with specialist skills. Other options will become attractive if nurses do not show interest in significant expansions in their functions.

The existing examples of nurses in expanded roles are impressive. The rationale for expansions to date, and for further expansion, is equally impressive. The examples and rationale should not be ignored.

The least-desirable future is one in which nothing changes. The current manner in which health care professionals are utilized is unfair and uneconomical. Current arrangements cannot deliver the greatest possible volume of necessary health care with the health care dollars which are available, and they perpetuate professional discrimination.

The preferred future includes cooperative, continuing, broad and saleable progress towards delivery of care by the professionals who can deliver an acceptable quality of care at the lowest cost.

In this time of change, all professionals have a choice. In an address to the annual meeting of the Canadian Physiotherapy Association in Saskatoon in 1992, Nancy McKay, President, described the two main choices:

> "For some, the intense scrutiny and dramatic change now bombarding our social and health care systems elicits defensiveness, fear and protectionism. The Canadian Physiotherapy Association views it as a time of opportunity; a time to set a new course through strategic planning; a time of exploring uncharted frontiers of the future as we

pursue a new vision for the physiotherapy profession; a time to exercise confident leadership in making our preferred future a reality."

If all professions make the same choice, the future will bring an increase in the adequacy of our publicly funded health care despite a continued decline in public expenditures on health care.

The Thirteen Controlled Acts Identified in the Regulated Health Professions Act (RHPA), Ontario

The extent to which each self-governing health care profession in Ontario is authorized by law to perform one or more of the controlled acts is spelled out in the relevant "professions" Act. Providers who are not authorized by law to perform a particular procedure may still have that procedure delegated to them by a professional who is legally authorized to provide it.

Each controlled act is described below. The descriptions are less detailed than in the legislation.

A summary of the extent to which each profession has authority to perform controlled acts is presented in Table 13.1.

Controlled act #1: Communicating a diagnosis

This section of the Act appears to try (unsuccessfully) to satisfy two incompatible positions. It tries to respond to a physician wish for continued very special status while also allowing better utilization of the skills of other professionals.

The RHPA makes a distinction between the authority to assess a patient and the authority to transmit a diagnosis to a patient.

The ability of many professions to assess a patient has been accepted. The Act does not comment on who is allowed to make a diagnosis, but perhaps it can be assumed that if a professional is authorized to assess a patient then that professional is also authorized to establish a tentative or firm diagnosis.

Only physicians, however, were given unlimited authority to "transmit a diagnosis" to a patient. Dentists, chiropractors, podiatrists, psychologists and optometrists were given limited authority to discuss diagnoses with patients. Other professionals were authorized to assess patients and treat patients, but not authorized to "transmit a diagnosis". (The Ontario Minister of Health is currently considering granting selected nurse practitioners limited authority to transmit selected diagnoses to patients.)

Nurse practitioners, physiotherapists, audiologists, speech language pathologists, chiropodists and midwives cannot legally transmit a diagnosis to a patient, although all can legally assess a patient and then provide treatment on the basis of the assessment. This legislated restriction on the discussion of diagnoses appears to be incompatible with the duty of all health care professionals to give information to patients, offer diagnostic and therapeutic alternatives, invite patient direction regarding which treatment to implement, and involve the patient in developing a care plan. It is assumed that nurse practitioners, chiropodists and other professionals routinely ignore the impractical and unacceptable limitations imposed by the various Acts governing specific professions.

Chiropodists in Ontario, for example, are legally able to see patients as independent practitioners. There is no need for the patient to have seen a physician first. The Chiropody Act defines the practice of chiropody as: "the assessment of the foot and the treatment and prevention of diseases, disorders and dysfunctions of the foot by therapeutic, orthotic or palliative means." Chiropodists are, therefore, legally able to examine a person's feet and treat many of the common conditions which are found, e.g., planters warts, callouses and ingrown toenails. To be allowed to treat and not be allowed to tell the patient what is being treated is quite strange.

Speech language pathologists offer another example. Ontario Bill 44, the professional Act governing speech language pathologists, defines the practice of speech language pathology as the assessment of speech and language functions and the treatment and prevention of speech language dysfunction and disorders. Despite the legal right to treat and diagnose, the law does not allow a speech language pathologist to communicate a diagnosis to a patient.

It can only be hoped that other provinces will pass legislation which is more logical and more in keeping with the rights of patients.

The process by which physicians, audiologists, physiotherapists, nurses, podiatrists, chiropodists and others evaluate a patient and choose a diagnosis is quite similar. All take a history, do a physical examination, analyze objective findings, review laboratory and other test results, make a list of possible diagnoses and then select the most probable diagnosis. Having reached a firm or a tentative diagnosis every professional should then, with the involvement of the patient, identify the most desired course of action. The new legislation which will surely be introduced in many provinces should legally legitimize the processes which all health care professions already follow. In Ontario, amendments to many of the Acts governing specific professions should be made.

The RHPA in Ontario represents a giant step forward in the evolution of health care legislation and care delivery, but, with respect to the legal right to establish a diagnosis and discuss it with a patient, Ontario is still much like the rest of the provinces. A number of professional groups in Ontario have asked for legislative changes which correct the existing anomalies, but the College of Physicians and Surgeons, the Advisory Council and the Minister have largely opposed the requested changes. It is a shame to force professionals to choose between obeying the law and delivering health care appropriately.

In opposing requests for permission to communicate a diagnosis, the College of Physicians and Surgeons stated that approval of such requests should not be given "unless practitioners of that profession receive education and clinical training comparable to that – of physicians." (CPSO *Member's Dialogue*, September 1995, p. 7.) Assuming that the comparison is between family physicians and other professionals, the condition is reasonable. If the comparison was made, it would be found that specialized personnel such as physiotherapists, midwives, clinical specialist nurses, medical social workers and paramedics receive more academic and practical training in their respective fields than do most family physicians. In addition, the restricted practices of each of these professionals means that as time passes their competence quickly improves. Five years after graduation, each of these professionals will, in their field, have increased the gap in competence between themselves and most family physicians. But most of them will still not legally be able to communicate a diagnosis to a patient.

Limits on the communication of a diagnosis produce ethical problems for professionals. The Rules of Conduct of the Canadian Physiotherapy Association, for example, require that physiotherapists determine and communicate a clinical diagnosis. Physiotherapists also must use a diagnosis when seeking informed consent from a client (Ontario Physiotherapy Association 1989 submission to the Ontario Health Professions Legislative Review). In addition, funding agencies, including the Ministry of Health, require physiotherapists to provide diagnoses on claims submitted for payment. The Ministry accepts the ability of the physiotherapist to establish a diagnosis but will not allow the diagnosis to be discussed with the patient.

Controlled act #2: Performing a procedure below the dermis or mucous membrane, or on or below the surface of the cornea or teeth

Ten professions are authorized to perform some of these acts in some or all situations. Physicians have unlimited authority.

Controlled act #3: Setting or casting a fracture or dislocation

This act can be performed only by physicians (with unlimited authority) and dentists (limited authority).

Controlled act #4: Moving the spine beyond the individuals usual range of motion using a low amplitude thrust

Chiropractors, physicians and physiotherapists are authorized to perform this act.

Controlled act #5: Administering a substance by injection or inhalation

Physicians, nurses, midwives, radiology technologists, respiratory therapists and dentists have unlimited authority. Podiatrists and chiropodists have limited authority.

Controlled act #6: Putting a hand, finger or instrument beyond specified points in the ear, nose, throat, urethra, vulva, rectum, or artificial body opening

Physicians and nurses - unlimited authority. Radiology technologists, midwives, chiropractors, physiotherapists and respiratory therapists - limited authority.

Controlled act #7: Applying or ordering application of any form of energy

This controlled act governs the use of, or the ordering of, such diagnostic tools as X-ray. Physicians and dentists have unlimited authority. Chiropractors and optometrists have limited authority.

Controlled act #8: Prescribing, dispensing, selling or compounding a drug

Physicians have unlimited authority. Midwives, dentists, podiatrists and chiropodists have limited prescribing authority. Pharmacists have full dispensing, compounding and selling authority.

Controlled act #9: Prescribing or dispensing lenses or eye glasses other than simple magnifying devices

Physicians and optometrists have unlimited authority.

Controlled act #10: Prescribing a hearing aid

Audiologists and physicians have unlimited authority.

Controlled act #11: Fitting or dispensing a dental prosthesis or device

Dentists - unlimited authority. Denturists and dental hygienists - limited authority.

Controlled act #12: Managing labour or delivering a baby

Physicians and midwives - unlimited authority.

Controlled act #13: Doing allergy testing

Limited to physicians.

Table 13.1

Professional Functions in Ontario, 1994
(as defined in the Regulated Health Professions Act)

Controlled Acts

Health	#1	#2	#3	#4	#5	#6	#7	#8	#9
Profession	Diag	Proc	Frac	Jnts	Injn	Orif	Ener	Drgs	Eyes
Audiologist	-	-	-	-	-	-	-	-	-
Speech Lang Path-	-		-	-	-	-	-	-	-
Podiatry	*	*	-	-	*	-	-	*	-
Chiropody	-	*	-	-	*	-	-	*	-
Chiropractor	*	-	-	All	-	*	*	-	-
Dent Hygienist	-	*	-	-	-	-	-	-	-
Dent Tech'ist	-	-	-	-	-	-	-	-	-

Dentist	*	*	*	-	All	-	All	*	-
Denturist	-	-	-	-	-	-	-	-	-
Dietician	-	-	-	-	-	-	-	-	-
Mass Ther	-	-	-	-	-	-	-	-	-
Med Lab Tech	-	*	-	-	-	-	-	-	-
Med Rad Tech	-	*	-	-	All	*	-	-	-
Midwife	-	*	-	-		*	-	*	-
Nurse	-	*	-	-	All	All	-	-	-
Occ Therapist	-	-	-	-	-	-	-	-	-
Optician	-	-	-	-	-	-	-	-	-
Optometrist	*	-	-	-	-	-	*	-	All
Pharmacist	-	-	-	-	-	-	-	*	-
Physician		All	All	All	All	All	All	All	All	All
Physioth'ist	-	-	-	All	-	*	-	-	-
Psychologist	*	-	-	-	-	-	-	-	-
Resp ther'ist	-	*	-	-	All	*	-	-	-

Table 13.1 (continued)

Professional Functions in Ontario, 1994

Controlled Acts

Health Profession	#10 Hearing	#11 Dental Prosth	#12 Pregnancy	#13 Allergy Test
Audiologist	All	-	-	-
Speech Lang Path	-	-	-	-
Podiatry	-	-	-	-
Chiropody	-	-	-	-
Chiropractor	-	-	-	-
Dent Hygienist	-	*	-	-
Dent Tech'ist	-	-	-	-
Dentist	-	All	-	-
Denturist	-	*	-	-
Dietician	-	-	-	-
Mass Ther	-	-	-	-
Med Lab Tech	-	-	-	-
Med Rad Tech	-	-	-	-
Midwife	-	-	All	-
Nurse	-	-	-	-
Occ Therapist	-	-	-	-
Optician	-	-	-	-
Optometrist	-	-	-	-
Pharmacist	-	-	-	-
Physician	All	-	All	All\
Physioth'ist	-	-	-	-
Psychologist	-	-	-	-
Resp ther'ist	-	-	-	-

All - indicates that the profession has unlimited authority to perform all forms of the controlled act and in all situations.

* - indicates that the authorization given to the professional for performance of the controlled act is limited in some way.

Speech language pathologists, dental technologists, dieticians, massage therapists, occupational therapists and opticians are not authorized to perform any of the controlled acts.

Index

D

E

F

U

United States, 5, 7, 55, 56, 58, 72, 95, 100, 106, 109, 114, 116, 118, 124
University of Alberta, 89
University of Toronto, 58, 81
University of Waterloo, 114
urology, 56, 118-119
user fees, 25, 74, 138
users, 18-19, 31, 64, 66, 72, 110, 124, 133
– priorities of, 24
– rights of, 28-29

V

Victorian Order of Nurses, 10, 56

X

X-ray technologists (see radiology technologists)